Rerum Novarum

Encyclical Letter of Pope Leo XIII on the condition of the working classes

Centenary Study Edition: with introduction and notes by Joseph Kirwan

Catholic Truth Society

First published 1983 by the
Incorporated Catholic Truth Society
38–40 Eccleston Square
London SW1V 1PD

ISBN 0 85183 524 4

AC

Printed by the Ludo Press Ltd, London SW18 3DG

Contents

My thanks go to my son, David, for his help.
His Latin is better than mine.

Joseph Kirwan

References

In the Preface and Translator's notes there are numerous references to two collections of documents, Arthur F. Utz, *La Doctrine Sociale de l'Eglise à travers les Siècles* (4 vols Beauchesne, Paris), referred to as Utz, *Doctrine*, and A. F. Utz, F. F. Groner & A. Savignat, *Relations Humaines et Société Contemporaine* (3 vols eds St Paul, Fribourg/Paris), referred to as Utz, *Relations*. *Acta Apostolicae Sedis* is referred to as *AAS*.

The following documents referred to in the text are published by the Catholic Truth Society:

Casti Connubii	Do 113
Divini Redemptoris	S 335
Gaudium et Spes	Do 363
Laborem Exercens	S 355
Mater et Magistra	S 259
Octogesima Adveniens	S 288
Pacem in Terris	272 1
Populorum Progressio	S 273
Quadragesimo Anno	S 105

Preface

It is commonly asserted that Pope Leo XIII's most famous encyclical came at least forty years late. Such a statement reveals a misunderstanding of the relationship between papal teaching on social issues and the world which is called upon to apply the teaching. Before a pope can make a realistic call for a social change the bases for that change must already exist in society. By the time *Rerum novarum* appeared the opportunity for effecting change had come. By then the teaching of a pope would be listened to.

This is perhaps another way of saying that a papal encyclical does not so much point to the future as tell people what the current position is. This point was expressed by Leo XIII himself when, having been pressed by his private secretary to take up a position on some social question and reminded of his own pastoral letters when he was a cardinal archbishop, he replied: 'A pastoral letter ought to prepare the ground; an encyclical ought to find it already cultivated' (related in Utz, *Doctrine*, p.xxix).

The revolution with which *Rerum novarum* is concerned (the term 'rerum novarum' means 'of revolution') was already well under way by 1891. The industrial revolution which ushered in the modern age is dated from about 1780 and the shape of that age was already clear by 1850, by which time revolutionary political changes were also in train. So vast and rapid a pace of change posed difficult problems for men whose office forbade them to speak lightly, the more so in that they could hardly but find much of what was happening repugnant in the extreme. Christians who were faced with the actuality of mass migration

i

from countryside to town and from cottage industry to factory and mine had first to experiment with possible answers to the new problems before a definitive teaching could emerge.

Writing, then, in 1891, Pope Leo XIII dealt not with one revolution, but with three: the first, that which the Liberals had made; the second, that which the Socialists threatened to make; the third, that which the Christians ought to be making. The Liberals had divided people into two classes, separated by a great gulf. On one side stood a small and rich group of those who owned the means of production–the capitalists–and on the other the multitude of poor, unpropertied and utterly dependent labourers–the workers–a mass on whom the rich had laid 'a yoke little better than that of slavery itself' (2). The Socialists promised to cure the Liberal evils by destroying the capitalist class together with the religious, moral and civil order which was supposed to be indissolubly bound up with it. Ownership of all the means of production would be transferred to the state and the unpropertied would remain as weak or even weaker than before. The Christians should renew men's witness to Christ, restore ownership to the unpropertied, return to the state its power to intervene to protect the weak against the strong, and obtain full recognition to the right of men to associate freely for common purposes and, in particular, of working men to form unions to defend themselves against their employers. They should work to root out the evils of Liberalism and afford no purchase to those of Socialism. But none of this could be possible unless the Church, which the first revolution had attacked and the second threatened to destroy, was restored to its rightful place in society and unless it filled that place adequately.

As the first two revolutions were bound up with the class war–its creation as a Liberal fact, its elaboration as a Socialist creed –so also was it Leo's central concern. It was his purpose, he said, 'to make clear the principles by mean of which the struggle can be broken off and ended, as equity and the facts of the case require' (1). Because the cause of the class war lay in the fact that 'working men are now left isolated and helpless, betrayed to the inhumanity of employers and the unbridled greed of competitors', the few into whose hands has been concentrated 'the hiring of labour and the management of industry and trade' (2), so its cure was to be found in action taken by the state to help the unpropertied and action taken by the unpropertied to help themselves. Essential to this self-help was the self-governing trade union, the aims of which must be the spiritual regeneration of the workers, the recovery for them of the wages of which they were being cheated and the access by them to property ownership for themselves and for their children (42).

The standards which Pope Leo set for his investigation – 'equity and the facts of the case' – are worth noting. Once it had been established what in fact was happening, the remedies proposed would have to satisfy the full extent of justice (cf. St Thomas Aquinas, *S. Theol.* II-II, Q.120, art.2). There is nothing mean or narrow in Pope Leo's view of what human society should and could be like.

It appears odd at first sight that, instead of proceeding at once to a positive analysis of facts and remedies, Pope Leo stepped to one side, as it were, to attack a 'false remedy', the abolition of private ownership of the means of production. This approach is logically correct, although it cost him some sympathy. He recognized the maldistribution of capital which put excessive power into the hand of a small minority as the proximate, material cause of the evils he denounced. The immediate, moral cause was the false principle of ownership on which men were acting, a principle which denies the duties which the right to own brings with it. The Socialists, on the contrary, saw the root of the evil as entirely material. They believed that it was private owner-ship in itself which destroyed the humanity both of those who owned and those who did not, and that no remedy was possible until the institution of property was destroyed and its very memory removed from men's minds. Leo was surely right in considering that there was no point in teaching how property should be used to serve mankind until he had rebutted the argument which asserted that private ownership of property could only harm mankind.

Nevertheless, many people have been alienated by his treat-ment of the question of property. It is true that the style of parts of his argument is reminiscent of Locke and other harbingers of Liberalism. Indeed, it would be surprising of he were not in-fluenced to some extent by Liberalism, given that he was a man of the nineteenth century. But such influence, if it did exist, was minor. He insists that private property must be safeguarded, but he asserts just as positively that 'where protection of private rights is concerned, special regard must be had for the poor and the weak'; and that 'as regards the protection of this world's goods, the first task is to save the wretched workers from the brutality of those who make use of human beings as mere instruments for the unrestrained acquisition of wealth' (30 & 33). He makes it clear that ownership is for use rather than enjoyment (5–7).

Despite these forthright statements, many people press the charge of Liberalism. Their view has been well put by Fr Arthur F. Utz, O.P.: 'There are solid grounds for asking whether the social structures at the origin of private property have not strongly influenced Catholic doctrine. Study of the documents of Pius IX and Leo XIII shows that the system of distribution of goods of their day served as the juridical basis for their theory and they did not think to ask if there might not be some other order which answered to human dignity . . . However, through his insistence on the social character of ownership Leo XIII tempered the individualism of his fundamental idea of private property. In doing this, he opened the way for the future evolution of thought about it. This social character, to which he drew attention, was strongly insisted upon by Pius XI in *Quadragesimo anno* and became in *Populorum progressio* the very basis of the distribution of goods. The division of goods among private owners thus recovers its original meaning as that was perceived by the Fathers of the Church: a human institution for a better and more peaceful sharing of terrestrial goods which, in themselves, belong to everybody' (*Doctrine*, pp.xxxiv–xxxv).

This judgment omits to consider the fact that Leo was writing primarily for Europe and North America, the developing lands of his day, and was intent on Christianizing their institutions. The Church has no mandate to condemn an institution which does not contradict the natural law. St Peter's, Rome, is not a university but a Mother Church. The occupant of its Chair does not deal in theories. His task is to lead men to Christ from where they are. Thus, while later popes have developed the teaching on property, all have continued to insist on the rightness and importance for person and society of the institution of private ownership of the means of production. Even John XXIII, whom many people seem to think came close to abandoning the principle, insisted that for any shift from private to public ownership the burden of proof lies on those who advocate the move (*Mater et magistra*,

117). As for Paul VI, who in *Populorum progressio* is thought by some to have gone even further than John XXIII in his thinking, the letter sent on his behalf by Cardinal Cicognani to the Chilean social study week of 1966 speaks for itself:

'The obstinacy of those people who defend a purely egoistical idea of ownership is most deplorable in the light of the strong defence which Catholic social teaching has made of this institution. In fact, a well ordered system of private ownership is a means of promoting human dignity and liberty, guaranteeing room for a family to live and breathe, and assuring personal security to the individual. It is indispensable for the exercise of personal initiative and, finally, it constitutes a right which is united intimately with human activity, "a right which derives its strength and virtue from the fruitfulness of labour," as John XXIII has said. It is for all these reasons that the Church has strongly defended the right of private ownership.' And Paul calls in Pius XII, John XXIII and the Second Vatican Council for support (Utz, *Doctrine*, XX, 60).

Those who accuse Leo XIII of the taint of Liberalism should consider what Paul VI said about Liberalism in his *Octogesima adveniens* (35): 'at the very root of philosophical Liberalism is an erroneous affirmation of the autonomy of the individual in his activity, his motivation and the exercise of his liberty.' It was against this that Leo laboured throughout his reign.

Before leaving this aspect of the encyclical it should be added that the Socialism to which Leo XIII gave his attention is closely akin to what we today call Communism or its variants in Leninism, Trotskyism and Maoism. Pius XI drew attention to the dividing line between the permissible and the impermissible factions of people who call themselves socialists (*Quadragesimo anno*, 111–126); and Paul VI discussed it in some detail (*Octogesima adveniens*, 26–34). But none of this is really relevant to Leo XIII's discussion of the socialist case against private ownership. In *Rerum novarum* he is not considering the broader socialist theory of man and of human society. He had already done that elsewhere (it is interesting to notice that Leo found the root of Socialism in Liberalism–cf. *Diuturnum illud*, 1881, in Utz, *Doctrine*, XXI, 18. Of interest also is that Pius XI accused Mussolini of having brought back socialism and made it look more attractive by 'the new uniform'–cf. *Non abbiamo bisogno*, in Utz, *Doctrine*, XXVI, 193). Any social theory which denied the legitimacy of private ownership of the means of production would fall foul not only of Leo's analysis, but also of the consistent teaching of all his successors.

Nevertheless, people reading *Rerum novarum* for the first time might do well to leave the section on the socialist remedy until after they have read and thought about the major argument in Part Two, with its emphasis on the need for a variety of measures from three agencies. From the *Church* must come witness to Christ's work in the world, in preaching and in action. From the *state* must come good general administration which minimizes the need for particular interventions, which, when they come, must be directed primarily towards help for the poor and especially for the unpropertied workers. And from the *workers themselves* must come self-help through solidarity and responsible action aimed at ending their proletarian condition. As for the *rich employers*, whose sinful behaviour is at the root of the evils to be amended, their part is to listen to the voice of the Church, to second the state's activities in favour of working-men and to work in harmony with the working-men's associations, even to the extent of forming with them joint associations.

Although Leo insists upon the duty of the state to intervene vigorously on behalf of the unpropertied workers, the thrust of his argument is in favour of non-state activity. The major part of the work of reform must lie with working-men themselves. Their solidarity is the key. In this lies their strength and they must be prepared to use that strength even to the extent of going on strike. It is obvious that Leo shrank from the idea of conflict and he certainly did not accept it as the active force for change in society (15). However, it is equally clear that when he called upon the state to prevent strikes from erupting he looked to it to exert pressure upon the employers. He did not intend to invite it to pass laws forbidding strikes (31–33).

In the event, working-men's associations have not done what Pope Leo expected of them. He argued that, although the state and the trade unions 'are born of one and the same principle, the natural sociability of men', there is a difference between them which is of kind, not of degree. The state is a public society, having the care of a good which is common to the whole community of the citizens. The trade union is a private society, having the care of a good which is common to its members but particular within the greater society which is the state (37–38). As long as the particular good of the trade union is kept in harmony with the common good of the political whole, it is the state's job to maintain conditions which enable the trade union to act freely. This relationship breaks down whenever the state seeks to absorb the trade union, making of it an instrument of government, or the trade union seeks to dominate the machinery of government. In either case, the public good of the whole and the private good of the part become so confused one with another that neither can be served (38).

In most of the world there are no free trade unions. Organizations which wear that label are either completely dominated by the state machine or have become integrated into it. It is only in the democracies, which are still largely Liberal in tone, that genuine trade unions exist; but in many of them the trade unions have become highly politicized and spend much of their effort in seeking to operate as partners of the state or even to dominate the state machine.

The major cause of this development has been the opposition of the trade unions to access by their members to individual ownership of the means of production. Apart from some syndicalist tendencies, which came to nothing, the unions in Britain and elsewhere have thrown their weight behind state ownership. Politicization of the unions has been an unavoidable consequence. When it is in the hands of the state that 'the hiring of labour and the management of industry and trade become concentrated', the trade unions must either fight government or dominate it.

Although the bias of the trade union attitude to property ownership runs opposite to that demanded by John XXIII (*Mater et magistra*, 117), the unions have not altogether condemned private ownership of the means of production and in fact tolerate a large element of it. However, the type of ownership they prefer is far removed from the widely spread property which the popes have advocated. They find it easier to deal with a few large-scale undertakings, where control is vested in the hands of a few, 'who for the most part are not the owners, but only the trustees and directors of invested funds' (*Quadragesimo anno*, 105). Pius XI added that these few administered the funds in their hands 'at their own good pleasure'; and it is a share in that 'good pleasure' which the unions seek for themselves.

Thus, the immense improvement in working-class standards of living which has been brought about since 1891 and particularly in the last thirty years, good though it is in itself, has not removed what Leo XIII saw as a major cause of the social evils he condemned. Pius XI was at pains to point out that 'proletarianism must be carefully distinguished from pauperism' (*Quadragesimo anno*, 60). If working-class standards of living were to be doubled and redoubled but workers still did not escape from their proletarian condition, the social order would remain grievously defective.

State behaviour also has been very different from that which Pope Leo envisaged. It must be kept in mind that in Section II B, 'The action of the state,' Leo is speaking of what would be done by the state as it ought to be (25). Of states as they are he did not have a high opinion. He found it necessary to remind governments that they must not meddle in matters which lie beyond their competence or arrogate to themselves powers which rob ordinary people of control of their lives (28–29); and he was well aware that state action is all too often suspect because of the preponderant influence of the rich and the powerful upon the public administration (35). Pius XI found it necessary to insist strongly that the state be reformed because of its tendency to arrogate to itself 'functions which can be performed efficiently by smaller and lower societies' (*Quadragesimo anno*, 79). In that connection, attention should be given to the very wide range of duties which Pope Leo proposed for the trade unions (43). In his day and for many years afterwards many of these tasks were performed by them and by other working-class associations, such as the friendly societies (for which Beveridge wanted, in vain, to keep a role: *Social Insurance and Allied Services*, para. 379–380). However, as part of the magnification of the role of the state which was consequent upon their preference for public ownership of the means of production, the trade unions have surrendered most of these since 1945.

While Leo insisted that the state had a duty to intervene on behalf of the weak against the strong, he maintained also that intervention should be strictly limited and general rather than particular. In the event, state activity has become virtually limitless–ubiquitous and more and more arbitrary. Leo demanded that state care be impartial, according to the rule of distributive justice, and this, for him, meant particular care for the unpropertied workers and for the poor and the weak. Since it is 'only by the labour of working men that states grow rich' it is only fair that they be 'not themselves made wretched in every way'; while as regards the rich, they 'can use their wealth to protect themselves and have less need of the state's protection' (27, 29). The position reached today in the so-called Welfare State is very different. Not only does most of public provision of 'welfare' go to the well-to-do (the state doing for them what they can do for themselves), but also they actually enjoy preference over the poor. The evidence for this state of affairs is conclusive. Brian Abel-Smith, a sociologist by no means unfavourable to state welfare provision, remarked nearly twenty-five years ago that 'the main effect of the post-war development . . . has been to provide free social services to the middle classes'. Wherever we look, whether at medical care, education, housing or public transport, the poor come off worse than the well-to-do and the poorest come off worst of all. On two counts, the state today stands in flat contradiction to the state which Pope Leo envisaged. In doing for people what they could do for themselves and particularly in making provision for the better-off it is acting where he thought it ought not to act; and in failing to make particularly good provision for the poor it is failing in what he regarded as one of its major tasks.

Meantime, the scourge of inflation which has continued without interruption for more than forty years, destroys the small savings of the poor, transferring them to the state and to the wealthy owners of real property, and constitutes a tax which is levied without any regard for ability to pay–two matters about which Pope Leo expressed great concern (17 & 35).

There can be no doubting the immense amount of good that has been done by the work of Pope Leo XIII and of his successors in the see of St Peter to demarcate the spheres of public and private social action and to awaken men's consciences to their duties towards others and their responsibilities for themselves. Nevertheless, it would be idle to pretend that in the three spheres which to Leo XIII were of the first importance–a much wider spread of private ownership of the means of production; vigorous social action by trade unions and other such associations; and 'impartial' and strictly limited state activity–the management of affairs has taken a very different direction from that he envisaged. There are not a few who would say that this is because his diagnosis and his remedies were mistaken. However, not one of his successors has chosen to differ from him on any of these points, but has rather referred men back to his teaching on them.

It is not only the state and the trade unions which have failed to act in accordance with Pope Leo's intentions for them. The Church in Rome has not been wanting in its teaching and urging, but most other local churches have been less vigorous. Leo urged that 'all who are in holy orders must bring to the work their full strength of mind and body' (45). What this entails was made explicit by Pope Benedict XV in a letter to the Bishop of Bergamo in 1920: 'Let no member of the clergy imagine that such activity is foreign to the priestly ministry because it has to do with economic affairs. It is enough that here is a field in which souls are in danger. We ask, therefore, that priests consider it to be one of their obligations to devote themselves to the greatest possible extent to social science and the social movement, by study, by watchfulness and by action; and to collaborate in every way with those who exercise a healthy influence in this area with regard to the general good.' This injunction was repeated by Pius XI in his letter to the Bishop of Lille in defence of trade unions in 1929 (Utz, *Doctrine*, XV, 15; XIX, 54). Despite some outstanding examples of obedience to these behests, as far as this country is concerned those papal letters have been virtually dead letters. We are in a vicious circle: ignorance of the social teaching of the popes drives men to other teaching while those who should be giving sound instruction stand by helplessly because they have not been taught.

There remains one part of the teaching of *Rerum novarum* at which we must look: the just wage. This we can do briefly here because it is dealt with in some detail in the Appendix and in the notes on Justice and on the Just Wage. All that needs to be said here is that, despite the heading to paragraph 34, it is a mistake to look in this encyclical for a full treatment of wage justice. Leo XIII did not set out to offer a full statement. Two elements are of importance generally. He accepts implicitly the existence of a market for labour services and the social value of differential wages as incentives to men to meet society's needs (14). He insists explicitly that, although the state must step in to protect weak workers against strong employers (the discussion of the 'just wage' comes within the section on state intervention), wage bargaining is primarily a matter for associations of workers and employers (34; 43–44). The cardinal matter of his teaching is much more basic. It is that a society fails to satisfy 'natural justice'–i.e. offends against the Creator, the Father of us all–if it establishes a regime in which multitudes of men have only their labour services whereby they can live and yet cannot obtain the means of existence because the payment made to them is insufficient. He thus meets head-on the argument that insufficiency of wages is often 'in the nature of things'. The nature of things is God's provision for mankind; and it is men's duty so to arrange their affairs as not to stand in the way of God's providence.

Concerning this translation

In this new English version of Pope Leo XIII's most famous encyclical I have set out to bring the style–admirable in its Victorian rotundity–into line with current English usage. At the same time, I have taken the opportunity to remove some errors which have marred our English version for ninety years. There is one point on which I have felt constrained to make what might be considered a major change in a matter which is certainly not of style nor, narrowly speaking, of error. This is the translation of the words *locupletes* and *proletarii*.

In the existing English version these are translated simply as 'rich' and 'poor'. The same is done in the French version in Utz's *La Doctrine Sociale de l'Eglise à travers les Siècles*. The German version in *Texte zur katholischen Soziallehre*, edited by Fr O. von Nell-Breuning, S.J., has 'rich' for *locupletes*, but 'unpropertied' *(Besitzlos)* for *proletarii*. Likewise, the Italian version put out by the Gregorian Press in Padua has *ricchi* and *proletarii*.

I have chosen to translate *locupletes* as 'wealthy owners of the means of production' and *proletarii* as 'the unpropertied workers' or, simply, 'the unpropertied', or as 'poor unpropertied workers' –depending on the context. That this should be done seems to me to be of considerable importance for a proper understanding of the encyclical.

By derivation, the word *locupletes* means those rich in land and cattle, which are the major means of production in a primitive society. In view of the contexts in which Leo XIII uses the word it seems to me inconceivable that he did not use it deliberately to distinguish rich owners of the means of production from the rich generally speaking. *Locupletes* is not the word for 'rich' which comes immediately to mind; and in passages where he is speaking of the rich generally Leo uses *divites* and *opulenti*. *Proletarii*, on the other hand, are not merely poor, nor even necessarily poor. They are propertyless.

Locupletes is used in eleven paragraphs and in seven of these places it is used in juxtaposition to *proletarii*. The contrast between the propertied and the unpropertied in the process of production is plainly deliberate. In every case there is a reference to the class division and the class war. In paragraphs 15 and 16 the reference is explicit. The other places where *locupletes* and *proletarii* are juxtaposed are paragraphs 1, 13, 17, 27, 45 – significantly including the first and the last in the encyclical. There are four occasions when *locupletes* is used without *proletarii* occurring in the same passage: paragraphs 3, 18, 24, 43. In 3 the socialist assault on private property is introduced; and since Leo was obviously aware that it was ownership of the means of production that the socialists attacked, the use of *locupletes* here is significant. In 18 the Pope speaks of the duties of the rich in the virtue of charity; however, in 16 and 17 he had been speaking of their duties in justice towards the *proletarii* and it seems reasonable to conclude that in 18 he has the same people in mind, on both sides of the class divide. In 24 Leo is speaking of the tasks of the Church, *locupletium et indigentium communis parens*, but at the beginning of the paragraph he says that these tasks are to be undertaken *ut bene habeant proletarii*. It would not be far-fetched to say that this is a case of juxtaposition of the two terms. In 43 the Pope is discussing the functions of trade unions. Speaking of the way in which the early Christians, for much the greatest part the poorest of the poor, won the affection of the rich and the powerful *(locupletium et potentium)*, he says that they did this by showing themselves to be 'energetic, hardworking, peaceful, tenacious of justice and above all of charity'. These are the *proletarii*, without a doubt; and this conclusion is made the more certain by the insertion of the passage into a discourse on the functions, duties and rights of a trade union.

The final point in favour of my rendering is that wherever these words occur together, and in other places also, Leo XIII is talking of the divide in society not merely between rich and poor, but specifically between 'a great mass of unpropertied workers', *proletarii*, and those 'who have been able to lay' upon them 'a yoke little better than that of slavery itself', *locupletes*. To translate one word simply as 'rich' and the other simply as 'poor' is surely to rob *Rerum novarum* of much of its point. It removes the detonator from the bomb.

Joseph Kirwan

RERUM NOVARUM

Encyclical Letter of Pope Leo XIII on the condition of the working classes

INTRODUCTION:

THE WORSENED CONDITION OF THE WORKERS

1. The nations of the world have for long been disturbed by the
    lust for revolution and it was to be expected that once
eagerness for change had been aroused it would spread from the
field of politics into the related sphere of economics.

The coming of new industrial growth with the application of
new techniques; of changed relationships between employers
and employed; of immense wealth for a small number and deepest poverty for the multitude; of greater self-reliance and closer
collaboration of the workers among themselves; and, finally, of a
worsening of morals; from all of these changes has come an
explosive struggle. The desperate anxiety which has seized upon
men's minds shows how much is at stake. In learned circles, in
business meetings, in popular assemblies, in legislative bodies, in
councils of government, everywhere men meet there is deep
concern about what is happening. No question is of more pressing
importance at the present time, none more strongly grips the
attention of mankind.

And so, venerable brethren, just as on former occasions when,
for the sake of the Church and the common weal, we thought it
opportune to address to you letters on political power, human
liberty, the Christian constitution of states, and other matters of
a similar kind, so also now we find ourselves drawn to write in
like manner about the condition of the workers.

We have already touched upon this question more than once, as occasion offered. However, consciousness of our apostolic office urges us to treat of it in this letter more fully and more explicitly. Our purpose is to make clear the principles by means of which the struggle can be broken off and ended, as equity and the facts of the case require. The case is a difficult one to disentangle and not without risk. It is not easy to assess the rights and duties which ought to govern relationships between the wealthy owners of the means of production, who supply capital, and the unpropertied workers, who supply labour, even without the danger presented by the unceasing efforts of violent and deceitful men to steer the masses away from right judgment and to foment civil discord.

The state of the social question

2. However that may be, it is clearly universally agreed that the interests of the people at the bottom of the social scale must be consulted promptly, as befits their plight. For the most part, they are tossed about helplessly and disastrously in conditions of pitiable and utterly undeserved misery. The old working men's guilds were abolished in the last century and no other means of protection was provided in their place. At the same time, all trace of the religion of our fathers was stripped from government and the law. And so it comes about that working men are now left isolated and helpless, betrayed to the inhumanity of employers and the unbridled greed of competitors. Voracious usury makes matters worse, an evil condemned frequently by the Church but nevertheless still practised in deceptive ways by avaricious men. In addition to all this, the hiring of labour and the management of industry and trade have become concentrated into the hands of a few, so that a tiny group of extravagantly rich men have been able to lay upon a great multitude of unpropertied workers a yoke little better than that of slavery itself.

I THE FALSE REMEDY: SOCIALISM

3. While inciting the needy to envy the wealthy owners of the means of production, the socialists argue that the remedy for this evil is the abolition of private property. Individual possessions

2

should become common property, they say, to be administered either by local authorities or by central government. In this transference of property from the private to the public sphere they claim to have found a cure for present ills which will lead to an equitable distribution of capital and income. Their device is ill-adapted to its purpose. It will not end the conflict; it will do harm to the working class; and it is, moreover, greatly unjust. It will do violence to lawful owners, divert government from its proper tasks and cause utter confusion in the state.

i. Socialism is of no use to the workers

4.   It is easy to see that anyone who does anything of any kind for pay does it primarily to get something as his own, something that belongs to him and to nobody else. He hires out his strength and skill to get possession of what he must have to satisfy his human needs. In working for a wage he works also for a full and perfect right to use his earnings as seems good to him. If, therefore, a man spends less on consumption and uses what he saves to buy a farm, that farm is his wage in another form, as much at his disposal as was the wage itself. It is precisely in this power of disposal that ownership consists, whether the property be in real estate or in movable goods. It follows that when socialists endeavour to transfer privately owned goods into common ownership they worsen the condition of all wage-earners. By taking away from them freedom to dispose of their wages they rob them of all hope and opportunity of increasing their possessions and bettering their condition.

ii. Socialism is unjust to individuals and families alike

5.   What is even more serious is that the remedy proposed is plainly unjust, since to possess property privately as his own is a right which a man receives from nature.

In this consideration is to be found one of the greatest differences between man and the rest of the animal creation. Brute beasts do not govern themselves. They are guided and controlled by two natural instincts: one keeps them on the alert, ready to display their strength and capacity for action; the other stimulates and at the same time regulates their individual desires. By one instinct they are led to protect their own lives, by the other to

3

propagate their species. Both purposes are served by the use of things which lie ready to hand, a condition which prevents any further development since it is only by their senses and what their senses perceive that they are moved. Man's nature is very different. At least as much as the rest of the animal creation he has full and perfect possession of animal faculties and therefore also of the enjoyment of material things. But even at its highest level, animal nature cannot set bounds to human nature, so far inferior is the one to the other. The animal nature is made to answer the call of the human nature and be obedient to it. What is most remarkable about us and distinguishes us, what classifies man as man and sets him apart from the brute creation, is the possession of mind or reason. It is because he is the only animal possessed of reason that there must be attributed to man the right not only to use things as all animals do, but also to have and to hold them in settled and permanent possession; and that applies not only to goods which are used up in their using, but also to goods which continue to give service over time.

The settled ownership of property is from the natural law

6.   This becomes even clearer when we make a deeper study of human nature in itself. Man's ability to understand an indefinitely large number of objects enables him to link the present with the future. Since he also has mastery over his own acts, he can govern himself by his own foresight and judgment, subject always to the eternal law, the guidance of God whose providence extends to all things. It follows that he has freedom to choose whatever course of action he judges to be in his own best interest, not only for the passing moment but also into the future. And from that it follows that it is right and proper for a man to have ownership, not only of the fruits of the earth, but also of the earth itself, because of his awareness that the earth is the source from which his future needs will be supplied. Because his needs are forever recurring—satisfied today, they are as pressing tomorrow—nature must have given to man access to a stable source of supply, one that is always at his disposition and on which he might expect to draw perennially. It is only the earth with its fruitfulness which can satisfy this requirement of permanency.

There is no case for introducing the providence of the state. Man is older than the state. Before any state came into existence,

4

man had already received from nature the right to make provision for his life and livelihood.

7. An objection to private ownership cannot be based upon the fact that God has given the earth to the whole human race for them to use and enjoy. In giving the earth to mankind in general he does not intend that all should exercise dominion over it indiscriminately. It is because he does not assign any part of it to anyone in particular, but leaves this question to be settled by man's industry and established national customs, that he is said to have given it in general. Besides, however it is distributed among individuals, the earth does not cease to serve the needs which are common to all men. There is no one who does not feed upon the produce of the fields. People without capital supply labour. Thus it may truly be said that the universal means of providing the necessities and comforts of life consists in labour, whether it is applied to a man's own land or in some type of industry, earning a wage which can have no other source than the manifold fruits of the earth, for which it is exchanged.

All this affords further proof that it is fully in accordance with nature to own property privately. The truth is that it is only when men cultivate it skilfully that the earth provides in plenty all that men need for the preservation of life and still more for its higher development. Thus, when a man expends the activity of his mind and the strength of his body in procuring the goods of nature he makes his own that part of nature's resources which he brings to completion, leaving on it, as it were, in some form, the imprint of himself. This being so, it cannot but be right for him to possess that part as his very own, nor can it be lawful for anyone to violate that right in any way.

8. It is amazing that some people dissent from arguments as powerful as these and seek to resurrect bad opinions long since outworn. Enjoyment only of the different products of the soil is all they are willing to concede to a private person. They flatly deny the existence of any right of freehold possession, whether of the land on which a man has built or of a farm which he has cultivated. They do not see that in making these denials they defraud a man of part of the produce of his labour. For the soil which is cultivated with toil and skill is greatly changed in condition: the wilderness is made productive, the infertile fruitful.

5

That which has improved the soil becomes so completely mingled with it as to inhere in it and become to a large extent utterly inseparable from it. Does justice allow any man to seize and enjoy something which another man has stained with his sweat? As effects follow their cause, so is it right for the fruit of labour to belong to those who have given their labour. It is with good reason, then, that the common opinion of mankind has found no merit in the dissenting opinions of a few. Making a close study of nature, men have found in nature's law the basis for a distribution of goods and for private ownership and have been fully convinced that these are in the highest degree in conformity with the nature of man and with peace and tranquillity. Practice has sanctioned this conclusion throughout the ages. It is confirmed and enforced by the civil laws, which, when they are just, receive their binding force from the natural law. The authority of the Decalogue adds its sanction, with its strict prohibition against any coveting of what belongs to another: 'You shall not covet your neighbour's wife, nor shall you set your heart on his house, his field, his servant–man or woman–his ox, his donkey or anything which is his' (Deut. 5:21).

Relations between families and the state are falsified

9.   The importance of rights of this kind which inhere in individual human beings is much better understood when they are looked at in the light of their connexion with and appropriateness to the obligations imposed on men by their family relationships. It is indisputable that everyone is completely free to choose between following Christ's counsel on virginity or committing himself to the bonds of matrimony when he decides upon a state of life. No human law can take away the original natural right of a man to marry or in any way impose limits on the principal purpose of marriage ordained by God's authority from the beginning: 'Increase and multiply' (Gen. 1:28). And so we have the family, the society of the household, which, small though it is, is a true society and older than any state; one therefore which must have its own rights and duties which depend not at all upon the state. Thus, the right of ownership, which we have seen to be given by nature to individual persons, must belong also to a man in his capacity of head of a family. That right is all the stronger inasmuch as the human personality is further developed in the family group.

10.   A most sacred law of nature ordains that the head of a
      family should provide for the necessities and comforts of
the children he has begotten. That same nature leads him to want
to provide for his children–who recall and in some sense extend
his personality–a reasonable degree of protection against ill-
fortune in life's uncertain course. This he can do only by leaving
income yielding property to his children as his heirs. As we have
said, the family is a true society equally with the state and, like
the state, it possesses its own source of government, the authority
of the father. Provided that it stays within the bounds set for it by
its own special purpose, the family has for this reason at least
equal rights with the state to choose and employ whatever is
necessary for its rightful life and liberty. We say, at least equal
rights. Inasmuch as the domestic household precedes the state,
both as an idea and as a fact, it must also have prior rights and
duties which are more immediately grounded in nature. Detes-
tation of political society would quickly take the place of desire
for it if citizens, families, found that when they entered upon it
their rights were rendered less secure and they were hindered
rather than helped.

11.   It follows that to want to see the state's power arbitrarily at
      work within the intimacy of households is to make a great
and pernicious mistake. Of course, when a family happens to be
in a state of great distress, helpless and utterly unable to escape
from its predicament, it is right that its pressing need be met by
public aid. After all, every family is a part of the state. Similarly,
when within a family there is grave dispute about mutual rights, it
is for the public authority to insist upon each party giving to the
other its due. In doing this the state does not rob citizens of their
rights, but rather strengthens them and supports them as it
should. However, rulers must stop at this point. Nature does not
permit them to go further. Its origin being where human life itself
begins, a father's authority is such that it can be neither abolished
nor absorbed by the state. 'Children are something of the father'
and in some sense an extension of his personality. Strictly speaking, it is not of themselves but by virtue of the family into which
they are born that children enter into and partake in civil society.
And precisely because 'children are naturally something of their
father . . . they are held under the care of their parents until they
acquire the use of free will' (St Thomas, *S. Theol.* II–II, Q.10,

art.12). Thus, when socialists set aside parental care and put that of the state in its place they offend against natural justice and dissolve the bonds of family life.

iii. Socialism is injurious to society itself

12. The harm goes further than injustice. Exceedingly great disturbance and upset would afflict all classes. Close behind would come hard and hateful servitude for the citizens. The door would be thrown open to mutual envy, detraction and dissension. All incentive for individuals to exercise their ingenuity and skill would be removed and the very founts of wealth dry up. The dream of equality would become a reality of equal want and degradation for all. None would be spared. From this it is plain to see that the socialist doctrine of common ownership ought to be altogether repudiated. It harms those it is meant to help; it denies to individuals their rights; it throws the administration of public affairs into disorder; it disturbs the peace. The conclusion is inescapable. All who set out to improve the conditions of the masses must start from the fundamental principle that private possessions must be held inviolate. That being established, let us proceed to an explanation of where the sought-for remedy is to be found.

II THE TRUE REMEDY: CONCERTED MEASURES

A. The action of the Church

13. We approach this matter with confidence, as we are fully entitled to do, since no good solution to the problem can be found without recourse to religion and the Church. Since the care of religion and of those matters for which the Church has responsibility falls principally to us, continued silence on our part would be seen as neglect of duty. Undoubtedly, there is need for others besides ourselves to bend their efforts to the cause: members of governments, employers and wealthy owners of the means of production, and finally those whose cause we are pleading, the people without property. Nevertheless, we do not hesitate to insist that whatever men may choose to do will be in

vain if they leave out the Church. Evidently it is the Church which draws from the Gospel teaching strong enough to end the conflict or, at the very least, make it less bitter; and she it is who tries by her injunctions not merely to inform men's minds, but also to guide the life and morals of every one of them. She has highly efficient organizations which promote better conditions for the unpropertied; she urges all classes to work together in thought and action to produce the best possible solution to the difficulties of the workers; she argues that the state ought to apply its administrative and legislative authority to the same end, to the extent that the situation requires.

i. Inequalities and the hardships of labour are unavoidable

14.   The first point to be made is that men must put up with the human predicament: in civil society it is not possible for those at the bottom to be equal with those at the top. Socialists are violently opposed to this, but they struggle in vain against the nature of things. The differences which exist naturally between men are great and many. There is no equality in talent, or skill, or health, or strength, and these unavoidable differences lead of themselves to inequalities of fortune. This is clearly of advantage both to individuals and to society. A community needs to have within it different capacities for action and a variety of services at its disposal; and men are most impelled to supply these by the differences of their condition.

As regards manual work, even in the state of innocence men would not have been wholly idle; but what they would then have chosen freely for the pleasure it gave them became, after the Fall, something to which necessity compelled them to submit, in painful atonement for their sin. 'Accursed be the soil because of you. With suffering shall you get your food from it every day of your life' (Gen. 3:17). In like manner, men may not look for an end to their bitter legacy in this life. The burden of the ill-effects of sin lies heavily on them, harsh and difficult to bear. There is no escape for any man to the end of his days. To suffer and endure is the lot of men; and whatever means they use and however much they try, no art, no force can free their society from this painful condition. Anyone who claims to be able to rid the common people of all pain and sorrow and to bring them peace and a life of never-ending pleasure lies outrageously. He sets out a false prospectus which can lead only to an eruption of evils even greater than those men suffer now. The best course for men to follow is to accept reality and seek elsewhere for suitable means to alleviate their troubles, as we have pointed out.

ii. Concord is necessary

15.   In the subject under discussion it is a great mistake to imagine that class is spontaneously hostile to class, as if nature had matched together the wealthy owners of the means of production and the unpropertied workers to persist stubbornly in laying wildly about each other. This picture is so far removed from truth and reason as to be directly contrary to both. Just as the different parts of the body unite to form a whole so well proportioned as to be called symmetrical, so also nature has decreed that in the state these twin classes should correspond to each other in concord and create an equilibrium. Each stands entirely in need of the other: there can be no capital without labour, nor labour without capital. Concord begets order and beauty, whereas a continuation of conflict leads inevitably to barbarity and wild confusion. Christian institutions are possessed of marvellous and many-sided strength which enables them to put an end to conflict and to cut away its roots.

iii. The class conflict can be calmed

Justice

16.   By constantly recalling both parties to the duties they owe each other, and especially to their obligations in justice, the teaching of religion, of which the Church is the interpreter and guardian, is immensely well qualified to bring together the wealthy owners of the means of production and the men without property. Among the obligations of justice which bind the unpropertied worker are: to fulfil faithfully and completely whatever contract of employment he has freely and justly made; to do no damage to the property nor harm to the persons of his employers; to refrain from the use of force in defence of his interests and from inciting civil discord; to avoid the company of men of evil principles who use artful promises of great results to raise extravagant hopes which can end only in vain regrets and heavy loss. For his part, the rich employer must not treat his workers as

though they were his slaves, but must reverence them as men who are his equals in personal dignity and made the more noble by their Christian calling. Both natural reason and Christian philosophy agree that it does not shame a man to engage in a profitable occupation. Rather does it do him credit, for it provides him with an honourable means of livelihood. What is truly shameful and inhuman is to misuse men as instruments for gain and to value them only as so much mere energy and strength. There is an obligation to keep in view the religious needs of unpropertied men and the good of their souls. Employers must see to it, therefore, that the worker has time for his religious duties; that he is not exposed to morally corrupting influences and occasions of sin; and that he is not seduced from his domestic duties and a wise use of his earnings. Furthermore, employers must not impose tasks which overtax a man's strength or are of a kind which is unfitted to a worker's age and sex.

17. However, among the major duties of employers the most important is to give to each and every man what is just. Of course, there are many matters to be kept in mind when a just standard of wages is being considered; but wealthy owners of the means of production and employers must never forget that both divine and human law forbid them to squeeze the poor and wretched for the sake of gain or to profit from the helplessness of others. To defraud a man of the wage which is his due is to commit a grievously sinful act which cries out to heaven for vengeance. 'Labourers mowed your fields, and you cheated them—listen to the wages that you kept back, calling out; realize that the cries of the reapers have reached the ears of the Lord of hosts' (James 5:4). Lastly, the wealthy owners of the means of production must take scrupulous care not to harm in any way the savings of the unpropertied, whether by force, or fraud, or usurious dealings; and this the more so both because their poverty makes them ill-equipped to counter injustice and because what few possessions they have should be held the more sacred the scantier they are.[1]

Might not compliance with these rules of conduct be able of itself to rob these differences of their force and utterly to remove their causes?

---

[1]See translator's note: Usury (pp.41–3).

Charity

18.   But the Church, with Jesus Christ for teacher and guide, seeks persistently for more than justice. She warns men that it is by keeping a more perfect rule that class becomes joined to class in the closest neighbourliness and friendship. We cannot understand and value the goods of this mortal life unless we have a clear vision of that other life of immortality. If we lose sight of that, we lose also and at once the true sense of virtue. Everything to do with our material world becomes lost in a mystery which no human mind can fathom. Nature and Christian dogma concur in teaching us the truth which forms the base on which the whole concept of religion rests: that it is only after we have left this life that we shall really begin to live. It is not for the fleeting and the perishable, but for the heavenly and the eternal that God has created man. The earth he gives us as a place of exile, not a dwelling place. Abundance or lack of wealth and other things which men call good is of no importance for eternal happiness. How we use them is of the greatest importance. When Jesus Christ brought to us his plentiful redemption, he did not relieve us of the various sorrows which form so large a part of mortal life; he transformed them into incentives to virtue and occasions of merit. It is plain that no mortal being can come to possess the goods of eternity unless he follows in the blood-stained footprints of Jesus Christ. 'If we hold firm, then we shall reign with him' (2 Tim. 2:12). The labours and sufferings which he bore of his own free will have marvellously blunted the edge of all labour and suffering. He has made it easier to endure sorrows, not only by his example, but also by his grace and the hope of everlasting reward which he holds out to us. 'Yes, the troubles which are soon over, though they weigh little, train us for the carrying of a weight of eternal glory which is out of all proportion to them' (2 Cor. 4:17).

Therefore, the wealthy are warned that wealth brings neither freedom from sorrow nor help towards the happiness of eternity, to which indeed it is more of an obstacle (Mt. 19:23–4). Let the rich owners of the means of production tremble at the exceptional threats of Jesus Christ (Lk. 6:24–5): God will demand the strictest accounting for the use they make of their possessions.

The true advantage of riches

19.   Most excellent and of the greatest importance is the teaching on the use to be made of wealth which philosophy discovers incompletely but the Church gives clearly and perfectly. Moreover, she does this in such a way as to influence men's conduct as well as inform their minds. The fundamental point of this teaching is that the rightful possession of riches is to be distinguished from their rightful use. As has just been established, to own goods privately is a natural right of man; and to exercise that right, particularly in society, is not only good but entirely necessary. 'It is not only legitimate for a man to possess things as his own, it is even necessary for human life' (St Thomas, *S. Theol.* II–II, Q.66, art.2). And if the question be asked, 'How must possessions be used?', the Church replies without hesitation: 'No man is entitled to manage things merely for himself, he must do so in the interests of all, so that he is ready to share them with others in the case of necessity. This is why Paul writes to Timothy: "As for the rich of this world, charge them to be liberal and generous"' (St Thomas, *S. Theol., ibid.*). True, no one is commanded to provide aid for others out of what is required for his own needs and those of his household; or, rather, to hand over to others what he needs to provide a fitting standard for himself: 'Nobody should live unbecomingly' (St Thomas, *S. Theol.* II–II, Q.32, art.6). But when necessity and seemliness have been satisfied, there is the duty of using what is over to relieve the poor. 'Give alms from what you have' (Lk. 11:41). These are not duties of justice, except in extreme cases, but of Christian charity, duties which it is not right to have enforced by law. But prior to the laws and judgments of men there are the law and judgment of Christ, who in many ways recommends the habit of giving generously: 'There is more happiness in giving than in receiving' (Acts 20:35); and who will judge a kindness done or refused to the poor as a kindness done or refused to himself: 'In so far as you did this to one of the least of these brothers of mine, you did it to me' (Mt. 25:40).

   This teaching can be summarized thus: whoever has been generously supplied by God with either corporal and external goods or those of the spirit, possesses them for this purpose–to apply them equally to his own perfection and, in his role as a steward of divine providence, to the benefit of others. 'Let him who has a talent, therefore, be careful not to hide it; let him who enjoys abundance watch lest he fail in generosity to the poor; let him who possesses the skills of management be particularly careful to share them and their benefits with his neighbour' (St Gregory the Great, *Evang. Hom.* IX, n.7).

The innate dignity of poverty

20.   As for the poor, the Church teaches insistently that God sees no disgrace in poverty, nor cause for shame in having to work for a living. Christ our Lord confirmed this by his way of life, when for our salvation he who 'was rich became poor for our sake' (2 Cor. 8:9). He chose to be seen and thought of as the son of a carpenter, despite his being the Son of God and very God himself; and having done so, made no objection to spending a large part of his life at the carpenter's trade. 'Surely, this is the carpenter, the son of Mary?' (Mk 8:3). Contemplation of this divine example makes it easier to understand that a man's worth and nobility are found in his way of life, that is to say, his virtue; that virtue is the common inheritance of mankind, within easy reach of high and low, rich and unpropertied alike; and that the reward of eternal happiness is earned only by acts of virtue and service, by whomsoever they are performed. Indeed, the will of God himself seems to give preference to people who are particularly unfortunate. Jesus Christ proclaims formally that the poor are blessed ('Happy are the poor in spirit' Mt. 5:3); most lovingly he invites all those who labour and mourn to come to him, the source of comfort ('Come to me, all you who labour and are overburdened', Mt. 11:28); with loving care he clasps closely to himself the lowly and the oppressed. Knowledge of all this cannot but lower the pride of the well-to-do and lift up the heart of the poor man who is full of misery, turning the one to fellowship and the other to moderation in his desires. Thus, the separation which pride tends to create will be lessened in extent and it will not be difficult for the two classes willingly to join themselves together in bonds of friendship.

Christian brotherhood

21.   However, if they obey Christian teaching it will be the bond of brotherly love rather than of friendship that will unite them. They will then feel and understand the obvious truth that all men have the same Father, who is God the Creator; that all reach out for the same final good, who is God himself, who alone

14

can bring absolutely perfect happiness to both men and angels; that by the action of Jesus Christ all alike are redeemed and re-established in the dignity of sons of God, so that all might be bound together in fraternal love, brothers to one another as they are to Christ our Lord, 'the first born among many brothers'. The same benefits of nature and gifts of divine grace belong in common to the whole human race, without distinction, and only those who are unworthy will be disinherited. 'If we are children we are heirs as well: heirs of God and co-heirs with Christ' (Rom. 8:17).

Such is the scheme of rights and duties which Christian philosophy teaches. Where this teaching flourishes will not all strife quickly end?[1]

iv. There are positive steps to be taken

The spread of Christian teaching

22.   Not content with merely pointing out the way to set things right, the Church herself takes reform in hand. She commits herself entirely to educating men by her teaching and forming them by her discipline, and by the work of her bishops and priests she seeks to spread the life-giving waters of her doctrine to the furthest possible extent. She strives to inform minds and direct wills so that men will allow themselves to be ruled and guided by the discipline of God's teaching. It is in this, the principal matter of importance because on it depends all the good that is sought for, that the action of the Church is peculiarly effective; and this because the instruments she most uses to influence men's minds are given to her for that very purpose by Jesus Christ and derive their effectiveness from God. It is only instruments of this kind which can touch the innermost reaches of the heart and lead a man to put his duty first, to control his appetites, to love God and his neighbour with his whole heart and soul and to stamp out courageously all that stands in the way of a life of virtue.

The renewal of society

In matters of this sort it is enough to glance briefly at the pattern of antiquity. There is not the slightest doubt about the events we bring to mind. Civil society was renewed from its foundations by the teachings of Christianity. By virtue of this

---

[1]See translator's note: Christian philosophy (p.44).

renewal the human race was lifted up to better things, called back indeed from death to life, to a life more perfect than any known before and as good as any yet to come. The first cause and final end of these benefits is Jesus Christ: as all things come from him, so all must be brought back to him. Undoubtedly, as by the light of the Gospel tidings of the great mystery of the incarnation of the Word and of the redemption of mankind were spread throughout the world, the societies of men were permeated by the life of Jesus Christ, God and man, and imbued with his faith, his teaching and his laws. If the society of mankind is to be healed, it can be done only by a recall to Christian life and teaching. If societies in decay wish to be restored, the truest starting point is a return to their origins. The perfection of all associations consists in seeking and attaining the end for which they were established, and this will be done when all social activity springs from the same cause as that which gave societies birth. It is for this reason that to fall away from the original principles is to suffer corruption and to return to them is to have wholeness restored. This is true, not only of the whole body of the state but also of that class of citizens, by far the largest, who work for their living.

The promotion of a better standard of living

23.   It must not be thought that the Church's great concern with the care of souls leads her to neglect the affairs of this earthly and mortal life. She wants expressly to see the unpropertied workers emerge from their great poverty and better their condition; and what she wants, she works for. That she calls men to virtue and forms them in its practice is no small help of itself in that direction. Complete adherence to the code of Christian morals leads directly of itself to greater prosperity. It joins men with God, the ground and fount of all good things; it restrains an excessive appetite for material possessions and a thirst for pleasure, the twin plagues which often make even the rich man unhappy: 'The love of money is the root of all evils' (1 Tim. 6:10); it teaches contentment with a frugal standard of living, so that income from savings is available to meet misfortune and the vices which eat up not only small but exceedingly large fortunes and dissipate great inheritances are avoided.

24. In addition to this, moreover, the Church takes direct action to bring prosperity to the unpropertied by founding and fostering institutions which she knows will be conducive to their escape from poverty; and in this she has always been successful enough to wring praise even from her enemies. So deeply did the first Christians love one another that very many among them who were well-to-do stripped themselves of wealth to bring aid to those worse off: 'None of their members was ever in want' (Acts 4:34). The Apostles instituted the order of deacons to take charge of the daily distribution; and despite his burden of care for all the churches St Paul did not hesitate to undertake laborious journeys to bring alms to the poorer Christians. These sums of money, collected by the Christians by universal agreement, were called by Tertullian 'deposits of loving kindness' because 'they are used entirely to feed the needy when they are alive and bury them when they are dead, to care for poor orphans, aged servants and the shipwrecked' (*Apologia* II, 39). Thus there came gradually into existence an inheritance which the Church has looked after with scrupulous care as the property of the poor. She has always tried to collect funds to help them so as to spare them the humiliation of begging. Acting as the mother of the rich owners of the means of production and of the poor alike and drawing upon the great fount of love which she everywhere creates, the Church has founded congregations of religious and many other useful institutions which have done their work so well that there is hardly any kind of need for which help is not provided. There are many today who follow the example of the heathens of old and find fault with the Church for showing such great charity. They argue that state welfare benefits should be provided instead. But there is no human device which can take the place of this Christian charity, which thinks of nothing other than to bring help where it is needed. The Church alone possesses such virtue because its source is the heart of Jesus Christ himself. There is none other. And whoever cuts himself off from the Church wanders far from Christ.

25. However, it is not to be doubted that to do what needs to be done calls for everything that lies within men's powers. It is necessary for all who have a part to play to work and strain to do their share. As with the providence which governs the world so also here, we see that effects which depend upon a number of causes come about only when all are at work together.

B. The action of the state

The next step to take, therefore, is to ask what part of the remedy is to be looked for from the action of the state, it being understood that in this context 'state' does not refer to such examples as we find in practice in this country or in that, but to that which sound reasoning congruent with nature and the lessons of divine wisdom show to be good. All of this has been clearly explained in encyclicals on the Christian constitution of states.

i. The right of the state to intervene

26.   The first task of rulers is to make use of the whole system of laws and institutions to give assistance both generally and to particular classes. Statesmanship consists in making the structure and administrative functioning of the state conduce of themselves to public and private prosperity. Bringing this about is the particular function of those who govern. The prosperity of a state is best served where there are sound morals, well-ordered family life, regard for religion and justice, moderate taxes equitably levied, growing industry and trade, a flourishing agriculture, and other provisions of a like kind which it is generally agreed will contribute to the greater well-being and happiness of the citizens. By these means rulers can benefit other classes and at the same time be of the greatest help to the unpropertied. It is fully within their right to act thus and since by virtue of its office the state ought to care for the common good they are not to be accused of excessive interference. The greater the abundance of opportunities which arise out of this general care, the less will be the need to try other measures to help the workers.

Regard for the common good

27.   But there is another aspect to be considered which is of very great importance in this connection. The one purpose for which the state exists is common to the highest and the lowest within it. By nature, the right of the unpropertied men to citizenship is equal to that of the wealthy owners of the means of production, for they through their families are among the true and living parts which go to form the body of the state. Indeed, it can be added, in every actual state they are greatly in the majority. Since it would be utterly absurd to care for one section of citizens

and neglect another, it is evident that the public authority ought to take proper care to safeguard the lives and well-being of the unpropertied class. To fail in this would be to violate justice which bids us give to every man his due. As St Thomas has wisely said: 'As a part and the whole are identical in a sense, so too in a sense that which is of the whole is also of a part' (*S. Theol.* II–II, Q.61, art.1, ad.2). Consequently, not the least nor the lightest of the duties which fall to rulers in their regard for the common good, but that which comes first of all, is to keep inviolate the justice which is called distributive by caring impartially for each and every class of citizen.

Regard for the interests of the workers

However much it is necessary for all citizens without exception to make some contribution to the common good, which of itself benefits every individual, each enjoying his share,[1] it is not possible for everyone to contribute in the same way or to an equal extent. For a state to exist at all, or even be thought possible, there have to be differences of degree among its citizens and these will persist however much forms of government may change. It will always be necessary to find people who will devote themselves to public affairs, make the laws, dispense justice, and by their counsel and authority administer affairs of state and the conduct of war. Such people have a leading part to play and ought to be accorded pre-eminence in every state. Anyone can see that their labours make an immediate and invaluable contribution to the common good. Then there are those who are engaged in some kind of business. These do not serve the state in the same way and to the same extent and, valuable though their service is, it is less direct. Lastly, although it is obvious that the social good is principally a moral good, since it ought to be of such a kind that in enjoyment of it men are made better, nevertheless a characteristic of a well constituted state is an abundance of material goods, 'the use of which is necessary to virtuous action' (St Thomas, *De Regimine Principum*, I, xv). Such goods cannot be provided without the highly productive, skilled and painstaking labour of the unpropertied workers who are employed in farms and factories. So great is their vigour and efficiency in this regard that it may truly be said that it is only by the labour of

---

[1] See translator's note: The Common Good (pp.44–7).

working-men that states grow rich. Equity requires of the state, therefore, that it have particular regard for the unpropertied workers, so that those who bring so much of advantage to the community should themselves be well housed and clothed, enjoy greater comfort and suffer less hardship. Whence it follows that measures ought to be supported which are seen in some way to offer an improvement of the condition of the workers. Such solicitude is far from being harmful to others. Rather, it is greatly beneficial to the whole community, for it is of great importance to the state that those from whom such necessary goods proceed are not themselves made wretched in every way.

ii. The standards and limits of the state's right to intervene

The principle of intervention

28. We have said already that the state has no authority to swallow up either the individual or the family. To the extent that the common good is not endangered or any person hurt, justice requires full freedom of action for both. On those who govern lies the duty of caring for both the community and its parts. The community, because nature's charge to the ruling authority to maintain it makes care of the public welfare not only the supreme law of the state, but also its entire cause and the sole reason for its existence; the parts, because management of the state is to be used for the advantage of those who are governed, not of those who govern. Philosophy and the Christian faith concur in this conclusion. Since the power to rule originates in God and might be termed a participation in his supreme authority, the example to be followed is that of God's dominion which cares like a father for each individual creature as much as for the whole universe. The public authority must intervene, therefore, whenever the public interest or that of a particular class is harmed or endangered, provided that this is the only way to prevent or remove the evil.

The application of the principle of intervention

29. The maintenance of peace and order is of as much importance to the public as to private good. Its requirements are: the regulation of family life in accordance with God's commands and the law of nature; respect for and the fostering of religion; insistence upon the integrity of public and private morals

and on the sanctity of justice, so that no one shall hurt another with impunity; care for young citizens so that they can grow up strong enough to serve and, if need be, defend the state. Wherefore, should it happen that a strike or a lock-out threatens disorder; or the natural ties of the family are weakened among the unpropertied; or the practice of religion among the workers is harmed because time is not allowed to them for its observance; or the integrity of morality is endangered in the factories by indiscriminate mixing of the sexes or other evil practices which create occasions of sin; or the employing class imposes unjust burdens on the working class or afflicts them with conditions inconsistent with the dignity of the human person; or too great a burden of work damages health or has insufficient regard for sex and age; in all such cases it is plainly true that, within certain limits, the force and authority of the law must be brought to bear. The facts of each particular case determine the limits to the application of the law; but evidently, the law must not be asked to do more nor to proceed further than is necessary to put right what is wrong or to avert what threatens.

Rights must be held sacred wherever they exist. The public authority must enable every individual to maintain his right by providing for the prevention and punishment of transgressions. Where the protection of private rights is concerned, special regard must be had for the poor and weak. Rich people can use their wealth to protect themselves and have less need of the state's protection; but the mass of the poor have nothing of their own with which to defend themselves and have to depend above all upon the protection of the state. Because the wage-earners are numbered among the multitude of the poor, the state owes them particular care and protection.

iii. Particular occasions for intervention

Protection of private property

30. Particular attention must now be given to certain very important matters. At the head of the list is the duty to use the strength and protection of the law to safeguard private possessions. At the present time, when greed is rampant, it is of the greatest importance to keep the masses in the way of duty. It is permissible for people to try to better themselves provided that in doing so they commit no injustice, but neither justice nor reasons of

public advantage permit them to take what belongs to others and to pounce upon the fortunes of others in the name of some foolish uniformity. Of course, the great majority of the workers prefer to improve their condition by honest work without inflicting injury on any one; nevertheless, there are not a few who, steeped in false opinions and eager for revolution, seek by every means to foment trouble and urge others on to violence. The public authority should intervene to put a brake on the activities of rabble-rousers and thus protect workers from bad influences and legitimate owners of property from the risk of plunder.

Defence of labour: Strikes

31.　Hours that are too long, work that is too heavy, wages said to be too low, these are reasons usually given by workers when they go on strike. These stoppages are a frequent cause of serious inconvenience, hurt employers and employed alike, do harm to trade and damage the general public interest, bringing violence and disorder close and endangering peace. Everybody should be seeking a remedy. Much the best and most efficacious course is for the law to intervene in good time before trouble starts, to prevent it from erupting by removing the causes of conflict between employers and workers.

Conditions of labour

32.　There are many matters of a like kind in which the worker needs the protection of the state. His spiritual good comes first. Good and desirable though this mortal life is in itself, it is not the ultimate end for which we are born. It is only the way and the means by which, through knowledge of the truth and love of the good, we reach the perfection of the life of the soul. It is upon the soul that is impressed the divine image and likeness and it is in it that resides the sovereignty by virtue of which man is commanded to rule over the whole of the lower creation and to use all the earth and the sea for his own needs. 'Be fruitful, multiply, fill the earth and conquer it. Be masters of the fish of the sea, the birds of heaven and all the living animals on earth' (Gen. 1:28). In this respect all men are equal. There is here no difference between rich and poor, between masters and servants, between rulers and ruled: 'all belong to the same Lord' (Rom. 10:12). Nor may anyone violate with impunity the dignity of man, whom God himself treats 'with great reverence', or to impede progress to that perfection which corresponds with the eternal life in heaven.

It follows that no man has the power freely to consent to treatment not in accordance with his nature and to deliver his soul into slavery. The rights which are at stake are not at a man's own disposition. They are duties owed to God and must be scrupulously observed. Hence the necessity of rest from work on holy days. Such rest is not to be thought of as indulgence in mere idleness; much less is it, as many would like it to be, an opportunity for spending money on vicious pursuits. It is to be a real rest from labour, hallowed by religion. When it is joined with religion, it withdraws a man from the daily round of work and business dealings and leaves him free to think about heavenly goods and pay to God the debt of adoration which is owing. Such, above all, is the nature of the seventh day of rest and the reason for it. This is what God decreed among the principal laws of the Old Testament: 'Remember the sabbath day and keep it holy' (Ex. 20:8); and what he taught by his own action, the mysterious rest which he took immediately after he had created man: 'He rested on the seventh day after all the work he had been doing' (Gen. 2:2).

33. As regards protection of this world's goods, the first task is to save the wretched workers from the brutality of those who make use of human beings as mere instruments for the unrestrained acquisition of wealth. It is evident that neither justice nor common humanity permits some men to impose upon others such a heavy burden of labour as will stupefy their minds and exhaust their bodies. A man's ability to work is limited, as is his nature, and there is a point beyond which he cannot go. He can develop his strength by training and use, but only if he obeys the rule of limited spells and frequent periods of rest. Care must be taken, therefore, not to lengthen the working day beyond a man's capacity. How much time there must be for rest depends upon the type of work, the circumstances of time and place and, particularly, the health of the workers. There must be appropriately shorter hours of work in occupations, such as mining for coal and quarrying iron and the like, where the burden of labour is particularly heavy and also injurious to health. Account should be taken also of the seasons of the year, for often what can be done easily at one time becomes quite impossible or extremely difficult at another. Finally, it is unjust to ask of a woman or a child work which is well within the capacity of a strong and

healthy adult man. Great care must be taken always to prevent the employment of children in factories until they are sufficiently mature in mind and body and character. Calls which are made too early upon the strength of youth can beat it down, like new-grown grass too tender to be trodden, and quite destroy all possibility of education. It is equally true that certain types of work are less suitable for women, who are adapted rather to domestic tasks. It is these which best safeguard their womanly virtue and most correspond to the bringing-up of children and the well-being of the family. The general rule is that the greater the burden of labour the greater must be the provision for rest and recuperation: what work has taken away, rest from work must restore. In any contract made between employers and employed there is always the explicit or implicit condition that opportunities must be provided for both rest and recuperation. Any other agreement would be unjust, for there is a duty never to ask on one side, nor promise on the other, neglect of the duties which a man owes either to God or to himself.

The just wage

34.   The subject we now approach is of equally great importance.

It is one which must be properly understood if we are not to offend against one party or the other. It is argued that, given that the scale of wages is decided by free agreement, it would appear that the employer fulfils the contract by paying the wage agreed upon, that nothing further is due from him and that injustice will be done only if the employer does not pay the full price or the worker does not perform the whole of his task. In these cases and not otherwise it would be right for the political authority to intervene and require each party to give to the other his due. This is an argument which a balanced judgment can neither entirely agree with nor easily accept. It does not take every consideration into account; and there is one consideration of the greatest importance which is omitted altogether. This is that to work is to exert oneself to obtain those things which are necessary for the various requirements of life and most of all for life itself. 'With sweat on your brow shall you eat your bread' (Gen. 3:9). Thus, human work has stamped upon it by nature, as it were, two marks peculiar to it. First, it is *personal*, because the force acting adheres to the person acting; and therefore it belongs entirely to the worker and is intended for his advantage. Second, it is *necessary*, because a man needs the results of his work to maintain himself in accordance with a command of nature itself which he must take particular care to obey. Were we to confine our attention to the personal aspect, we could take it for granted that the worker is free to agree to any rate of pay, however small. Since he works of his own free will, he is free to offer his work for a small payment, or for none at all. But this position changes radically when to the personal we join the necessary aspect of labour, as we must. For although they can be separated in theory, in practice the two are inseparable. The reality is that it is every man's duty to stay alive. To fail in that is a crime. Hence arises necessarily the right to obtain those things which are needed to sustain life; and it is only the wage for his labour which permits the man at the bottom of the ladder to exercise this right. Let workers and employer, therefore, make any bargains they like, and in particular agree freely about wages; nevertheless, there underlies a requirement of natural justice higher and older than any bargain voluntarily struck: the wage ought not to be in any way insufficient for the bodily needs of a temperate and well-behaved worker. If, having no alternative and fearing a worse evil, a workman is forced to accept harder conditions imposed by an employer or contractor, he is the victim of violence against which justice cries out. In these and similar cases–such, for instance, as the regulation of hours of labour in different industries or measures to safeguard health and safety at work–it is important to prevent the public authorities from thrusting themselves forward inconsiderately. Particularly because of the great variety of circumstances, times and places, it will be better to reserve such matters to the judgment of associations, of which more will be said later, or to find some other way by which the interests of wage-earners can be safeguarded. In the last resort appeal must be made to the help and protection of the state.

Zeal for the promotion of thrift

35.   If a worker earns a wage which enables him to make ample provision for the needs of himself, his wife and his children, he will find it easy to practise thrift. If he is sensible, does what nature itself advises him to do and cuts out excessive expenditure, he can contrive to acquire some little property. We have seen that effective efforts to put an end to the troubles facing us must start from the principle that the right to own privately must be

maintained absolutely. For that reason the law should support this right and do what it can to enable as many as possible of the people to choose to exercise it. Most valuable consequences must follow from such action, the foremost among them being a more equitable distribution of wealth. The forces of social change have split states between two classes separated by an enormous gulf. On one side stands the extremely powerful party, because extremely rich; which, being in possession of the whole of industry and trade, turns all means of production to the service of its own ends and is able to take no small part in the government of the state. On the other side stands the multitude of the weak, destitute of resources, filled with bitterness and ever ready to revolt. However, if the efforts of the people were aroused by the hope of acquiring something of what the soil contains, it would gradually come about that class would move closer to class and the gulf which separates the greatest wealth from the deepest poverty be removed. An additional benefit would be more abundant supplies of all the goods of the earth. When men work on what they know to be their own, they do so with more readiness and greater care. Indeed, they fall wholly in love with the land they cultivate and which yields them food and an abundance of other things for them and theirs. It is obvious how greatly this quickening of the will can add to the volume of production and the revenues of the state. And there is a third advantage to be looked for from this. Men prefer to remain in the land in which they were born and reared and they are less likely to leave it for foreign parts when it provides them with the means to obtain a better life.

However, one condition which must be satisfied if these benefits are to be obtained is that private means must not be exhausted by excessive taxation. Because the right to possess property privately is given by nature and not by human law, that law has no power to abolish it. All that the public authority may do is to regulate the use of property in keeping with the requirements of the common good. To take from private citizens under the guise of taxation more than is equitable is unjust and inhuman.

C. The action of associations

i. Everybody's collaboration is necessary

36.   Finally, employers and workers can do much themselves in
       this matter by means of institutions which can bring timely
aid to the needy and draw class closer to class. Examples of these
are mutual benefit societies; foundations of various kinds to
provide security for workers and their widows and orphans in
cases of sudden emergency, illness and death; and welfare
organizations which provide for the protection of children,
adolescents and older people.

But the most important are working-men's associations, the
aims of which include almost all of those listed above. The good
work done by the old guilds of artisans is well known. They
brought benefit to the members themselves and also did much to
develop the crafts, as many monuments show. Working-men's
associations have to be adapted now to the greater demands
which are made on people in an age of wider education and new
ways of life. It is gratifying that everywhere societies of this kind
are being formed, either by workers alone or by both classes
together, and it is greatly to be desired that they should become
both more numerous and more efficient. We have spoken of
them more than once and this is the place to demonstrate that
with their many advantages they exist of their own right and to
discuss how they should be organized and what they ought to do.

ii. There is a natural right of association

37.   Experience of his own weakness both impels and
       encourages a man to ally his forces with those of another.
As the Bible puts it: 'Better two than one by himself, since thus
their work is really profitable. If one should fall, the other helps
him up; but woe to the man by himself with no one to help him up
when he falls down' (Eccles. 4:9–10); and in another place:
'Brother helped by brother is a fortress, friends are like the bars
of a keep' (Prov. 18:19). Just as a man is led by this natural
propensity to associate with others in a political society, so also
he finds it advantageous to join with his fellows in other kinds of
societies, which though small and not independent are nevertheless true societies.

Because of their different immediate objectives there are many differences between these societies and the great society we call the state. The purpose for which the state exists concerns all the citizens as a whole because it comprises the common good—a good in which all and each have a right to participate in a proportionate degree. It is called a *public* society because in it 'men join themselves together to form a state' (St Thomas Aquinas, *Contra impugnantes Dei cultum et religionem*, c.II). By contrast, societies which are formed within the state are said to be *private*, and rightly so because their immediate purpose is the particular interest peculiar to their own members: 'A private society is one which is formed to attain private objects, as when two or three form an association to trade in common' (*ibid.*).

38. Although private societies exist within the state as parts of it, as it were, the state does not possess the power to make a general order against their existence. It is by virtue of the law of nature that men may enter into private societies and it is for the defence of that law, not for its destruction, that the state comes into being. If the state forbids its citizens to associate together it obviously makes war upon itself, for both it and the private associations are born of one and the same principle, the natural sociability of men. There will be occasions when the law may rightly intervene against private associations, as when some among them pursue policies which are plainly contrary to honesty, justice and the good of the state itself. In cases such as these the public authority may with justice prevent the formation of associations and dissolve them where they exist. However, great care must be taken lest the rights of the citizens be emptied of content and unreasonable regulations made under the pretence of public benefit. For laws have to be obeyed only when they accord with right reason and the eternal law of God.[1]

39. Here we bring to mind the confraternities of various kinds, the associations and religious orders which the authority of the Church and the holy will of Christian people have brought

---

[1] 'A human law has the force of law to the extent that it falls in with right reason: as such it derives from the eternal law. To the extent that it falls away from right reason it is called a wicked law: as such it has the quality of an abuse of law, rather than of law' (St Thomas, *S. Theol.* I–II, Q.93, art.3, ad.2).

into being. History tells us how much benefit they have been to the human race right up to our own day. Looked at solely in the light of reason, it is evident that societies of this kind have been formed by natural right because the purposes for which they have been established are good. As far as they affect religious matters it is to the Church alone that they are answerable. The rulers of the state, therefore, have no just ground on which to claim any right over them or to interfere in their administration. It is rather the duty of the state to defend and help them and shield them from harm when they have need of protection. However, what has been done, particularly in our own day, has been very different from this. By making them subject to civil law, denying their corporate status and seizing their property the state has in many places attacked communities of this nature and inflicted many injustices upon them. The Church had a right in that property, as also had the members of the associations, those who endowed them for their purposes and those for whose benefit they were endowed. We cannot withhold our objection to such unjust and wicked despoliation. We have all the more reason for complaint because the law proclaims freedom of association even while it is proscribing societies of Christian men and refusing to them, who are men of peace seeking only the general good, what it grants freely to others whose objectives are harmful to both religion and the state.

40.   Associations in immense variety and especially unions of workers are now more common than they have ever been. This is not the place to enquire into the origins of most of them, their aims or the methods they employ. There is plenty of evidence to confirm the opinion that many are in the hands of secret leaders and are used for purposes which are inconsistent with both Christian principles and the social good. They do all that they can to ensure that those who will not join them shall not eat. In this state of affairs Christian workers have but two alternatives: they can join these associations and greatly endanger their religion; or they can form their own and, with united strength, free themselves courageously from such injustice and intolerable oppression. That the second alternative must be chosen cannot be doubted by those who have no desire to see men's highest good put into extreme danger.

iii. The exceptional opportunity of the present time

41.   High praise is due to the many Catholics who have informed themselves, seen what is needed and tried to learn from experience by what honourable means they might be able to lead unpropertied workers to a better standard of living. They have taken up the workers' cause, seeking to raise the incomes of families and individuals, introduce equity into the relations between workers and employers and strengthen among both groups regard for duty and the teaching of the Gospel–teaching which inculcates moderation, forbids excess and safeguards harmony in the state between very differently situated men and organizations. We see eminent men coming together to learn from each other about these things and unite their forces to deal with them as effectively as possible. Others encourage different groups of workers to form useful associations, advise them, give them practical help and enable them to find suitable and well-paid employment. The bishops offer their goodwill and support; and under their authority and guidance many of the clergy, both secular and regular, work assiduously for the spiritual interests of the members of these associations. Nor is there any lack of help from Catholics who are rich. Many have voluntarily associated themselves with the wage-earners and have spent large sums in founding and widely extending fraternal societies by means of which it becomes easy for a worker to acquire by his labour not only present advantages but also provision for honourable support in later life. How greatly community affairs have been helped by such varied and willing activity is too well known to require emphasis. These associations give ground for hope for the future, provided that they continue to develop and to be prudently conducted. The state should protect them and the right they embody, but it must not intrude itself into their conduct of their own affairs. For the spirit which moves to life and action is fed from within and external force can all too easily crush it.

iv. The right to self-government

42.   An association has to be harmoniously organized and carefully administered if it is to arrive at agreed courses of action and a union of wills. Since citizens are possessed of a

power freely to join together in associations, they must also have a right to choose freely how they shall manage their affairs and how legislate so as to attain most effectively the purposes they have set before themselves. We do not consider it possible to set forth detailed rules for the constitution and administration of these self-governing societies. These are to be largely determined in the light of careful consideration of national characteristics, past experience, the nature and efficacy of the work to be done, the stage of economic development, and many other features peculiar to the time and place. What can be done is to enunciate a general law which holds good at all times: the constitution and administration of self-governing unions of workers must be such as will enable the societies to serve their purposes most speedily and completely and thus bring to their members as great as possible an increase in physical and spiritual well-being and access to property. It is clear that perfection of faith and morals ought to be seen as being of the first importance and it is to this end that the conduct of union affairs ought to be principally aimed. Unions managed otherwise must degenerate and become like those other societies which have no place for religion. What does it profit a man if through his union he obtains a plentiful supply of material goods but finds his soul imperilled by a lack of spiritual food? 'What, then, will a man gain if he wins the whole world and ruins his life?' (Mt. 16:26). Christ our Lord teaches us that this is the mark by which the Christian is to be distinguished from the heathen: 'It is the pagans who set their hearts on all these things . . . Set your hearts on his kingdom first, and on his righteousness, and all these things will be given you as well' (Mt. 6:32–3). Therefore, with God as their starting point let the unions make ample provision for the religious instruction of their members to give them a thorough awareness of what is due to God–what they ought to believe, what to hope for and what to do for the sake of their eternal salvation. Particularly great care must be taken to arm them against false ideas and corrupt men who would seduce them from their path. The worker is to be urged to the worship of God and the whole-hearted practice of religion, and in particular to the observance of the holy days. Let him be led to reverence and love the Church, the mother common to us all. Let him submit to her teaching and frequent the sacraments, the divine instruments for removing stains from his soul and preparing him for holiness.

v. Functions, duties and rights of associations

43. When societies found their laws upon religion they can easily establish mutual relations among their members which secure their peace and prosperity. Offices should be allocated so as best to serve the common purpose, particular care being taken to ensure that distinctions do not breed discord and that the duties are distributed intelligently and defined clearly. Harm to individuals will follow if this is not done. Common funds must be properly administered and the aid appropriate to the needs of individuals be settled beforehand. The rights and duties of employers are to be suitably reconciled with the rights and duties of workers. Should a member of either class think himself to be in any way injured, nothing would be better than that the laws of the association should provide for the appointment of a committee of honest and prudent men, members of the association, whose judgment will determine the issue. It is of the greatest importance also to provide for jobs to be readily obtainable at all times and for funds to be available to relieve the needs of individuals in cases of industrial accident, sickness, old age and any other cause of distress. The willing adoption of these means will enable these Catholic societies to meet the needs of the poor suitably and sufficiently and to bring desirable aid to the prosperity of the state. It is not rash to make provision for the future in the light of past experience. Times change, but it is remarkable how far conditions remain the same because God's providence governs all. He rules the course of events and turns it to serve the end he set before himself when he created the human race. We are told that in the early days of the Church it was cause for reproach against the Christians that the majority of them had to live precariously by manual labour or by begging for halfpence. But destitute of wealth and power though they were, they won the love of the wealthy owners of capital and the advocacy of the powerful. They showed themselves to be energetic, hardworking, peaceful, tenacious of justice and above all of charity to an exemplary degree. In the presence of that mode of life and behaviour all prejudice vanished, the disparagement of the illwilled was silenced and the untruths of long established superstition gave way gradually to Christian truth.

vi. The solution of the question of the workers is to be looked for from these associations

44.   The condition of the workers is the question of the hour. It will be answered one way or another, rationally or irrationally, and which way it goes is of the greatest importance to the state. Christian workers can easily end matters by forming associations, choosing wise leaders and entering upon the same road as that which their fathers followed with singular advantage to themselves and to the whole community. Great though the power of prejudiced opinion and of greed may be, unless the sense of what is right be deliberately and wickedly stifled the good will of the citizens will come spontaneously to turn more and more towards those whom they see to be industrious and moderate, putting justice before gain and the sacredness of duty before all things else. A further advantage to be looked for from such a course of action is the hope and opportunity of a better life that will be offered to workers who now either altogether despise the Christian faith or live contrary to its requirements. These men know for the most part that they have been fooled by false hopes and lying appearances. They feel themselves to be treated with great inhumanity by their greedy employers who regard them as no more than so many instruments of gain; but if they are members of a union it will be of one which has no love and no affection at its heart and is torn apart by the internal strife which is the perpetual accompaniment of proud and unbelieving poverty. Broken in spirit, worn out in body, how many wish to free themselves from servitude and humiliation! But though their desire is strong, human respect or the fear of hunger holds them back. The self-governing unions of Catholics can be of immense benefit to all of these men if they will invite them, hesitant though they are, to join them in their search for a solution to their difficulties and will receive them with faith and aid and comfort as they do so.

CONCLUSION

Charity is the queen of all the virtues

45.   You know, venerable brethren, who are the people who must work hard to settle this very difficult question and how they must act. Everyone must gird himself for his part of the

work and act with the utmost despatch to prevent delay from making utterly irremediable what is already so great an evil. Those who govern the state must make use of its laws and institutions; wealthy owners of the means of production and employers must be mindful of their duties; the unpropertied workers must exert themselves in legitimate ways in what is primarily their affair; and since, as we said at the beginning, religion alone is able totally to eradicate the evil, all men must be persuaded that the first thing they must do is to renew Christian morals. If that is not done even the wisest measures that can be devised to fit the case will fall short of their purpose.

As for the Church, whatever the time and circumstance her aid will never be looked for in vain. Those in whose hands lies the care of the general welfare must understand that the greater the freedom she is allowed, the more efficacious will be her action. All who are in holy orders must bring to the work their full strength of mind and body. Acting under your authority and inspired by your example, venerable brethren, they must never cease from setting before men of every class the pattern of life given to us by the Gospel. They must do all they can for the good of the people, particularly by way of strenuous efforts to nourish in themselves and to inspire in others the practice of charity, mistress and queen of all the virtues. For indeed it is from a great outpouring of charity that the desired results are principally to be looked for. It is of Christian charity that we speak, the virtue which sums up the whole Gospel law. It is this which makes a man ever and entirely ready to sacrifice himself for the good of others. It is this which is man's most effective antidote against worldly pride and immoderate love of self. It is of this that the Apostle Paul spoke in these words expressing its function and divine likeness: 'Love is always patient and kind; it is never jealous; love is never boastful or conceited; it is never rude or selfish; it does not take offence, and is not resentful. Love takes no pleasure in other people's sins but delights in the truth; it is always ready to excuse, to trust, to hope, and to endure whatever comes' (1 Cor. 13:4–7). As a pledge of God's mercies and a sign of our good-will towards each and every one of you, venerable brethren, and to your clergy and people, we lovingly bestow upon you the apostolic benediction in the Lord.

Given at St Peter's, Rome, the 15th day of May 1891, in the fourteenth year of our pontificate. LEO PP. XIII

Appendix

The reply from Rome to
three questions about wages

*When, in 1891, Cardinal Goossens, Archbishop of Malines, was
preparing for a Catholic congress in his archdiocese, he judged it
prudent to question Rome on the meaning to be given to the term
'natural justice' in paragraph 34 of* Rerum novarum. *An answer
came from Cardinal Rampolla, Papal Secretary of State. It is said,
however, that the author of the reply was Cardinal Zigliara, O.P.*

*(Translated from an appendix to a Latin edition of the encyclical
published in 1896 by Desclée, De Brouwer.)*

FIRST QUESTION: Does 'natural justice' mean commutative
justice, or natural equity?

REPLY: In the absence of any qualification, the sense is
'commutative justice'.

EXPLANATION: Since the work done by a workman is not at all
like merchandise, a wage is not the same as a price.

The work done by a workman is work which proceeds from
human freedom and for that reason gives ground of merit and
right for a wage or reward. Work is of a much higher rank than
trade, where the simple exchange of merchandise for its price
settles everything. Nevertheless, for the sake of clarifying the
issues the work done by a workman may be considered as a kind
of merchandise and the reward, or wage, as its price.

This is not unreasonable. Granted that the workman's work is
of a higher rank than merchandise, it yet possesses fully the
quality of merchandise by which it can be said to have its price.

The argument of St Thomas Aquinas is correct: 'That is called a wage which is given as due recompense to anyone for work or labour, as its price, as it were. Just as to pay the just price for any goods received from anyone is an act of justice, so also to pay a wage for work or labour is an act of justice' (*S. Theol.* I–II, Q.114, art.1).

Just like buying and selling, so also work and wages are acts of commutative justice which serve the interests which are common to the contracting parties, each one needing the goods or labour of the other and vice versa. Since what is for a common good ought not to lay a greater burden on one party than on the other but must obey the law of equality of value which is the hallmark of commutative justice, a contract of justice is established between employer and employed.

Now, as to the criterion by which equality of value between the manual work of the workman and the wage due from the employer ought to be established, we reply as follows.

It is said in the encyclical that the criterion is to be sought in the immediate goal of the workman, which lays upon him the natural duty or necessity of working to provide what is needed to maintain a suitable standard of life, this being the first and principal purpose for which manual work exists.

Therefore, whenever the work done is such that the workman for his part satisfies the immediate purpose of work by fulfilling the aforesaid natural duty and the wage paid falls short of that purpose (a suitable standard of living), where there are no other considerations or qualifying circumstances it has to be said that there is an objective inequality between the work done and the wage paid and, therefore, an offence against commutative justice.

However, in this matter there are generally two things to be considered:

First: The selling prices of goods are not exactly determined by the law of nature. They are settled by a sort of common estimation. The same is to be said in general about wages.

Hence, while the purpose of work (the provision of a suitable standard of living) is firmly maintained, common estimation will, or at any rate can, raise or lower wages by modest amounts without violating justice. In this respect wages are like the prices of traded goods, which by general estimation can be moderately raised or lowered without losing the equality of justice.

Second: In deciding the just equivalence of wage to manual work the common estimation looks not only to the quality and quantity of the work, but also to the time taken and the prices, which vary from place to place, of the goods which the workman has to buy to maintain his standard of living.

Therefore, finally, if the employer is greatly benefited by the work he can add something by way of a bonus, without offending against the justice due to the workman. Such spontaneous and praiseworthy conduct is a matter for his sense of honour and is not a question of justice.

Evidently, the same principles apply here as to just buying and selling.

SECOND QUESTION: Does an employer who pays a wage sufficient for the maintenance of the workman, but insufficient for the needs of his family, whether this be large—a wife and many children—or small, sin? If he does sin, against what virtue does he do so?

REPLY: 1. He does not sin against justice.
2. However, he may at times sin, either against charity or against common decency.

EXPLANATION: 1. From the fact that the equivalence of wage and work, put forward in the reply to the first question, is observed, it follows that the demands of commutative justice are fully met. The work is personal to the workman. It is done by him, not by his family. It relates to his family, not primarily and *per se*, but secondarily and *per accidens*, insofar as the workman shares with his family the wage he receives. Since in the event the family adds nothing to the work, justice does not demand that the wage due for the work be increased.

2. 'He may at times sin'—not generally and *per se*, but only *per accidens* and in certain cases. This is the reason for saying 'at times'.

A) 'Against charity'—not only in those ways in which a man can fail in charity towards his neighbour, but also in a special way.

The work done by a workman results in gain for his employer. Whenever the employer is bound by the precept of charity to undertake the obligations of charity in individual cases, he is bound to observe the order of charity. This order makes the workmen closer neighbours of their employer, because they labour daily to his advantage, than are other needy men who do nothing for him. For this reason, the employer who can exercise charity ought to give preference to his workers by paying to them out of charity more than the minimum which justice demands. Thus, their wages, augmented in this way by charity, will be brought closer to what is needed for the sustenance of their families.

This is the general, as it were, theoretical position. In practice, one should not judge rashly whether or not an employer has sinned against charity.

B) 'Against common decency'–the nature of which is to make repayment voluntarily, that is to say, not out of justice.

By 'decency' we do not mean gratitude for a kindness done. The work done by a workman is not a favour. Payment is made for it which is equal to its worth. But an employer can derive great benefit and gain from a workman's work, and when he actually does so he is bound by common decency to give something extra to the workman. In doing this he does more than strict duty requires. In this matter we refer again to the final sentences of the reply to Question One. It is clear enough that the worker has no sort of right to claim such a payment.

(Note by the editor, Fr F. X. Godts, C.SS.R.: This answer from Rome rejects the opinion that a family wage is due in commutative justice. As the interpretation of the encyclical given in this reply comes from the Holy See, it confirms that Leo XIII was emphatically not of the opinion that a family wage is due in commutative justice.)

THIRD QUESTION: Does an employer sin and, if so, how, if using neither force nor fraud he pays a wage smaller than the work performed deserves and a decent standard of living requires, it being understood that the workmen concerned take the jobs willingly and are satisfied with or freely consent to that wage?

REPLY: In the absence of any qualification, he sins against commutative justice.

EXPLANATION: As has been said, a workman's work is not, in the strict sense, a marketable commodity. Nevertheless, in order to get a clearer understanding in this matter it may be looked at as though it were. This is because, while its relationship with the wage due is that of equivalence, exactly as is the relationship between a commodity and its price, there is something more to it. Hence, we can properly argue from lesser to greater.

Other things being equal, when a thing is bought no one may pay less for it than common estimation, having due regard to time and place, reckons its worth to be.

The more certain is it, therefore, that it is impermissible, being contrary to justice, to pay a smaller wage than the work performed merits, that is, what is sufficient for a decent standard of living. On this question, see what the encyclical says.

We have used the phrase 'in the absence of any qualification'. There can be special cases in which employers may properly employ workers who are content with an inadequate wage. For instance, suppose that the employer would be left with nothing or with less than enough to maintain himself appropriately if he paid out an adequate wage—or, indeed, suppose he would be left with a loss.

In this and similar cases what appears on the face of it to be a question of justice is in fact one of charity, for that is the way in which the employer provides for himself and others. See the answer to the first question, where it is said that 'two things are to be considered'.

There is nothing in what the learned Cardinal de Lugo says which contradicts these explanations. Indeed, what he says supports them.

(Note by the editor, Fr F. X. Godts, C.SS.R.: In the appeal in which these three questions were put forward the following passage had been cited from Cardinal de Lugo's Disputatio 29, Tom. II, Tract. de Justitia, *sect.3, no.62: 'A wage which is insufficient for the maintenance of a servant is not always unjust, still less one which does not suffice for the maintenance of his wife and children. For, as Molina remarks, it can happen that his service is not worth such a wage and that many others are satisfied with it because they have other sources of income which make up for the smallness of the wage and enable them to provide for themselves.'*

Luis de Molina S.J. (1535-1600) and Cardinal John de Lugo S.J. (1583-1660) were members of a brilliant group of sixteenth and seventeenth century writers, mainly Spanish, who revitalized scholastic philosophy and theology.)

In 1895 Pope Leo XIII himself wrote to Cardinal Goossens and the other Belgian bishops. He offered no clarification of what had become a hotly disputed question. Instead, he asked the bishops, in his name, to 'admonish the Catholics not to engage in controversy and dispute among themselves in matters of this sort, whether by speeches or by pamphlets, nor make accusations against one another, nor presume to anticipate the judgment of the legitimate authority.'

Translator's notes

Usury (paragraphs 2 and 17)

The ecclesiatical definition of usury is contained in the encyclical *Vix pervenit* sent by Pope Benedict XIV to the bishops of Italy in 1745:

'The sin called usury is committed when a loan of money is made and on the sole ground of the loan the lender demands back from the borrower more than he has lent. In the nature of the case a man's duty is to give back only what he borrowed.'

The essence of the sin had already been stated more simply and graphically in the *Roman Catechism* of the Council of Trent (Pt III, c.8, no.11):

'To lend at usury is to sell the same thing twice, or more exactly to sell what does not exist.'

This is an echo of the teaching of St Thomas Aquinas (*S. Theol.* II–II, Q.78, art.1).

There are some things of which the use can be separated from the possession. Thus, a tenant has the use of a house while the owner retains possession (i.e. the right of disposal) and this right of disposal can be sold without any disturbance to the tenancy. The right to use the house and the right to dispose of the house are both real and can be sold and enjoyed separately. It is clear that in the case of a tenancy and all similar transactions there is a real service rendered for which a charge may lawfully be made.

There are other things of which the use cannot be separated from the possession (i.e. the right of disposal). Money is one of these. To lend money is to dispose of it. Indeed, there is no point in borrowing money unless the transaction gives the borrower the right to dispose of it; for money has no use other than its disposal. It is of use only because it is a means of exchange. To use it is necessarily to give to another person the right to dispose of it. Therefore, to charge for the right of disposal of money and for the right to use it is to charge twice for the same thing and to commit the sin of usury.

Usury is a form of dishonest trading and as such strikes at the basis of an economy. As Pope Pius XII pointed out: 'The purpose of the Church's legislation against usury was to ensure that commercial activity should be what it professed to be, a means of providing people with the best possible material goods and services' (Utz, *Relations*, no.2619). Those who have control of money and credit have it in their power to do immense harm to the public by inflicting what is in effect a private tax on industry. Hence the strong words used by Pius XI against those who would use their control of money to amass more wealth and power for themselves (*Quadragesimo anno*, 105–107).

Always present in usury is a taking advantage by the lender of the weakness of the borrower. Thus, the poor are peculiarly liable to be the victims of it. Oppressions and frauds which deprive them of some part of what is rightly theirs are often so close to usury in their manner and effect as for all practical purposes to be identifiable with it. Writing in 1881 Georg Ratzinger (*Die Volkswirtschaft*, pp.214–215) defined usury as 'the usurpation of another's property by means of a loan transaction' and remarked that 'the economically strong use usury to plunder the weak'. While 'the money loan was originally and still is in the language of today the essence of usury, there are other analogous transactions in which the property of another is usurped... In such transactions advantage is taken of the need, the carelessness and the inexperience of others to deprive them of their property and such conduct merits the name of usury.' Pope Leo was well aware of this argument.

Taking advantage of the weakness and ignorance of workers to compel or induce them to accept as wages less than they earn is one such analogous transaction and is clearly foremost in the mind of Pope Leo. When such oppression and fraud is wrapped up in a package of so-called 'services' from employer to employed which either do not exist at all or are charged for above their worth we have plain usury. Examples are payment in kind at exorbitant prices ('truck') and charges for advances on wages not yet due to be paid but already earned by the worker (cf. *Lev.* 19:13: 'You must not keep back the labourer's wage until next morning'). There is need always for the law to be scrupulous in the protection it gives to the poor against all such oppression.

It is obvious that a monetary economy is vastly more productive than is a barter economy. Money greatly facilitates exchange and thereby makes possible the high degree of specialization which is the secret of economic growth. Money is therefore an extremely powerful economic instrument. Many people argue that it ought therefore to be treated as though it were a capital good: i.e. sufficiently similar to a building or a machine to justify treating it as though, like them, it possessed the quality of having a use which can be separated from the right of disposal.

This argument that money is quasi-capital is an old one. In the fifteenth century St Antoninus of Florence was able to observe the development of a money economy in his native city and as Archbishop he gave much thought to the case that was being made for the lawfulness of charging for the use of money. He was forthright in his rejection of the argument.

To charge for the loan of money 'is unjust and contrary to the right of appropriation which a man acquires by his industry . . . Money as a means of exchange brings no profit except by the industry of him who disposes of it. Therefore, to sell to a borrower the profit he derives from his use of the money in trade and industry is nothing other than to sell him his own industry: and that is unnatural . . . It is the man who uses the money who makes the profit from his industry. Of itself money is not productive, as is obvious when it is kept in a safe. It is the borrower, not the lender, who makes the profit. A loan is a transfer of ownership (i.e. of disposal) and it is the borrower who runs the risk of loss and not the lender' (*S. Theol.* II, i.6).

Of course, when a lender inflicts an injury on himself by making a loan he may lawfully charge enough to compensate himself; and it can be generally accepted in a monetary economy that those who lend money lose thereby the opportunity of investing. Nevertheless, the Church's condemnation of usury is economically important because the compensation a lender may lawfully charge must ordinarily be less than the profit which investment offers because, as St Antoninus said so long ago, it is the borrower, not the lender, who runs the risk of loss.

Christian philosophy (paragraphs 16 and 21)

It is to be doubted if anybody now would speak of a philosophy being Christian. However, it is a term which fits the amalgam of theology and philosophy out of which Catholic social teaching has been built. And there is more to it than that. There can be said of *Rerum novarum* what the late Fr Thomas Gilby O.P. said of St Thomas Aquinas's ethical teaching in his *Summa Theologiae*: it 'is integrated in *sacra doctrina*, the teaching of the Gospel Revelation, and its full import can be appreciated only when it is read as a living part of this organic whole' (in the new Blackfriars edition of the *Summa*, Vol.18, *Principles of Morality*, p.xxi).

It is of interest to note that the Italian text (which is not a translation from the Latin but the basis from which the Latin text was made) has 'evangelical law' instead of 'Christian teaching' at the beginning of paragraph 21; and at the end of the paragraph it has 'contained in the Gospel' instead of 'which Christian philosophy teaches'. In the final stages of the preparation of his encyclical it must have become evident to Pope Leo XIII that there was much in his section on the Church's teaching which was not drawn directly from the Gospel. However, it would be a grave mistake to think that the change of wording indicates any loosening of the tie between Catholic social teaching and the Gospel message.

The common good (paragraphs 27 and 37)

The idea of the common good is central to Catholic social teaching. Many people seem to have great difficulty in grasping the idea – indeed, there are some philosophers who deny that it has any reality – so, perhaps, something may be gained from looking at what various popes have said about it.

First, commenting on the passage in paragraph 27 of *Rerum novarum*, Mgr Dell'Aqua, assistant Secretary of State to Pius XII, had this to say:

'These two principles show the respect which society owes to the human person on the one hand and the obligations which the person has with regard to the common good on the other. Guilty of an inexplicable withdrawal from everything that concerns the problems of society, many people often forget that co-operation in the service of the common good can go as far as participation in the management of public affairs. This duty is no longer the

44

privilege of a few; it ought to fall on everybody because of the responsibilities with which all are charged' (Utz, *Relations*, no.4683).

Pope Pius XII spoke often about the common good. Three of his definitions are these:

a) 'the external conditions necessary to the citizens as a whole for the development of their powers and duties, their material, intellectual and religious life' (Christmas 1942: Utz, *op.cit.*, no.244).

b) 'a worthy state of life, settled and peaceful for every class of people' (19 April 1945: Utz, *op.cit.*, no.102).

c) 'the establishment of normal and stable public affairs which make it easy for individuals and families to lead a worthy, regular and happy life according to God's law–this is the purpose and the rule of the state and its organs' (8 January 1947: Utz, *op.cit.*, no.3358).

The Fathers of the Second Vatican Council summed this up thus: the common good is 'all the circumstances of their social life which allow people, both as groups and as individuals, to attain more fully and freely to their own perfection' (*Gaudium et spes*, CTS Do 363, n.26).

Thus, great though the importance of material conditions is, the common good is first and foremost a question of the spirit. Thus Pius XII: 'The common good, for the sake of which civil authority is established, reaches its culminating point in the autonomous life of persons. Only a community of spiritual interests can hold men lastingly together' (6 December 1957: Utz, *op.cit.*, no.6397).

It is because men need the society of their fellows that the common good is so important. Thus, Pope Paul VI writing to the Spanish social study week in 1964: 'The common good of all societies, both the greater and the lesser, cannot be confined within purely technical limits. The common good is always the good of persons living in civil society by means of which they can reach a perfection which surpasses what is possible to them merely as individuals' (Utz, *Doctrine*, II, 247).

Thus, the common good for the sake of which the state exists does not consist in the aggrandisement of the state or of its functions. As Pius XI put it: 'The function of the state's authority is twofold: to protect and foster families and individuals, but neither to absorb them nor substitute itself for them' (Christian Education of Youth–*Divini illius magistri*–19).

On the other hand, the state's ability to protect and foster individuals and families depends upon the willingness of those individuals and families and other lesser groups within the state to keep the needs of the common good always in mind. 'Every group, without exception, ought to respect the needs and legitimate aspirations of other groups. Nay rather, all ought to keep in view the common good of the whole human family' (*Gaudium et spes*, 26).

As Leo XIII himself put it: 'Nature commands the citizen to make his contribution to general peace and prosperity, but it is human wisdom and not nature which determines the extent, manner and means of that contribution.' Thus, 'citizens in the upper classes should consider that they are not free to choose whether or not they will help those at the bottom of the ladder. They are obliged to do so. No one lives only for himself in society; each lives for all. If there are some who have nothing to contribute to the sum of the common good, those who can do so must contribute the more' (*Libertas praestantissimum*–'On Human Liberty'; and *Graves de communi*–'On Christian Democracy': in *The Pope and the People*, pp.76 and 177).

Thus, all men, all families and all lesser societies within the state owe a debt of duty to the common good of the state, while at the same time they and the state itself owe a debt of duty to the common good of all mankind. This all pervading debt is due in the virtue of general or social justice (St Thomas Aquinas, *S. Theol.* II–II, Q.58, art.5). About this virtue there is nothing static. It is lively in its appreciation of the need for changes in laws and institutions to meet changing needs and opportunities in society. Thus Pope Paul VI, in his allocution celebrating the 75th anniversary of *Rerum novarum*, spoke of 'the need to make the common good a reality by reforming existing legal standards where these do not make sufficient provision for an equitable sharing of the advantages and the burdens of life in society. In place of the idea of a static justice, protected by a positive law which is the guardian of a given legal order, there comes into the development of human society another idea of a dynamic justice which proceeds from the requirements of the natural law, of social justice' (Utz, *Doctrine*, XV, 24).

These quotations from the popes of recent times will perhaps give the student a better idea of what is meant by the common good and what that good implies by way of duty for each and every one of us, acting both as individuals and as members of families and societies. In the light of this teaching Mgr Dell'Aqua can be pardoned for finding withdrawal from concern for society's interests 'inexplicable'.

An extended consideration of the common good, its nature and its needs, is to be found in Pope John XXIII's *Mater et magistra*, Part Two, and his *Pacem in Terris* (CTS 3721), paras 53–66.

Justice (various places, especially paragraphs 27 and 34)

Pope Leo XIII was not engaged in writing a treatise on justice. He was hammering out a tract for the times. It was action he wanted, not debate. However, debate arose, as the questions put to Rome by the Archbishop of Malines indicate.

It is plain that Leo was not pleased, judging that the questioning would distract attention from the pressing need for action on behalf of the poverty stricken workers. In this he was right. But he failed in his attempts to halt debate. The questions his encyclical had raised proved to be too interesting as well as too important to be settled easily.

Some of these questions are discussed in the next note. As a preliminary to that enquiry we must here discuss the interesting and important question of what exactly Pope Leo meant by 'justice' in various contexts. Since justice is concerned with debts or obligations, we have to be able to specify who owes what to whom, and why, in every instance where justice is appealed to.

We may begin an examination of *Rerum novarum* from this angle with the reflection that Pope Leo was an active participant in the nineteenth century revival of scholastic and particularly thomistic thought. It is important for the student to have some knowledge of that thought.

The essentials of St Thomas Aquinas's thinking on justice are to be found in his *S. Theol.* II–II, QQ.57 to 62. (Those who can should refer to the excellent Volume 37, 'Justice', in the Blackfriars edition of the *Summa*, published by Eyre and Spottiswoode, which has the Latin text, an English translation and notes.)

'The subject matter of justice,' says St Thomas, 'is an external deed in so far as the doing or employing something is duly proportionate to another person' (Q.58, art.10). Commenting on this, Fr Thomas Gilby O.P. remarks that 'justice adds an equilibrium in our social environment through our outward deeds and use of things'. And St Thomas, commenting on the words of St Augustine of Hippo, 'Justice is love serving God alone', says: 'As loving our neighbour is comprised in loving God, so rendering to each his due is comprised in serving God' (Q.58, art.10, ad.6). What is due from one man to another can be a matter of convention, as with the rules of the road, but the more fundamental rights arise out of the very nature of the case and hence are called natural. No human law or human institution may touch them in such a way as to reduce or change them. It is to these that Pope Leo refers where he speaks of the obligations of *natural justice* (paras 11 and 34. See also *S. Theol.* II–II, Q.57, art.2).

Looking at the matter in detail, St Thomas remarks that 'justice directs a man in his relations with others. These relations fall under two heads, those with others considered as individuals and those with others as belonging to the community, inasmuch as he who serves the community serves all who come within it. Consequently, justice in its proper meaning can cover both. It is plain that all who are included in a community are related to it as parts to a whole. A part as such belongs to the whole and so any good of the part can be regulated within the good of the whole. Therefore, the good of each and every virtue, whether it orders a man's relationship to himself or to other individual persons, may be referred to the common good, to which justice directs. Thus, because justice directs a man to the common good, it can include the acts of all the virtues. Because of this, justice is called a general virtue' (Q.58, art.5).

This *general justice* Pius XI chose to call *social justice* (*Divini Redemptoris*, CTS 335, 53), partly to emphasise its social character, partly because the old name for it had been so abused as to have lost its meaning. Every particular virtue has a social aspect and it is general (social) justice which directs that aspect to the common good. 'As charity may be said to be a general virtue, inasmuch as it relates the acts of all the virtues to the divine good, so also may general justice be so called, inasmuch as it relates the acts of all the virtues to the common good' (Q.58, art.6).

This means that in all that a man does he is obliged in justice (social or general justice) to take account of the effect of his

48

actions on the common good of his community; indeed, he is obliged actively to seek that good. An act might be considered to be virtuous if it is looked at in isolation from the community, but be seen to be vicious when it is related to the circumstances in which it is performed. 'A man can be led by contempt for the common good into all manner of sins' (Q.59, art.1).

It is to be noted that this relationship between any particular virtue and general justice does not operate the other way round. An act against a particular virtue cannot be made virtuous by an appeal to its public benefit. This becomes obvious if we have a right idea of the meaning of the common good. Indeed, 'inasmuch as all vices are contrary to the common good they have the character of an injustice, as though injustice is their source' *(ibid.)*.

The fact that general (social) justice directs the acts of all the particular virtues to the common good does not make it identical with those virtues. 'Just as besides general justice there have to be other particular virtues which regulate a man's relationship with himself, like temperance and fortitude, so also there has to be a particular form of justice to regulate his dealings with another individual person' (Q.58, art.7).

A man's obligations of particular justice towards another person can arise either from his relationship to him in the course of trade, business or profession; or from his relationship to him by virtue of their membership of the same community. Out of the first relationship arise obligations of *commutative justice*– so-called from the Latin word 'commutare' meaning 'to exchange' (commutative justice might therefore more simply be called *exchange justice*). Out of the second relationship arise obligations of *distributive justice*, so-called because each member of a society ought to have a care for the equitable distribution of the burdens and benefits of the community (Q.61, art.1). This virtue of distributive justice is of principal importance to rulers (*Rerum novarum*, 27), but all must observe it to the extent that they can, in St Thomas's words, 'apportion proportionately to each his share from the common stock' *(ibid.)*. In this connection we should note also what St Thomas says of avarice: 'It is not possible for one man to enjoy extreme wealth without someone else suffering extreme want' (*II-II*, Q.118, art.1, ad.2).

Justice has always to do with some sort of equality: 'a work of ours is said to be just when it meets another on the level' (Q.57, art.1). This even-handed dealing differs according to the relationship out of which the obligation arises. With exchange justice, each party must give to the other (as closely as can be judged) the equal in value to what he has received. The equality required by the trading relationship is of things to things. With distributive justice the equality required is one of the proportionality of things to persons. Exchange justice pays no attention to the needs or merits of the parties to a transaction. Distributive justice is concerned entirely with respective need or merit (Q.61, art.4). This explains why, in paragraph 27, Pope Leo argues that impartial care for each and every class of citizen calls for special solicitude for the unpropertied workers; and in paragraph 29 that the rich can be left to look after themselves but the poor must have the state's protection.

There is one further point to be made. This has to do with equity. 'Laws that are rightly enacted fall short in cases when to observe them would be to offend against natural right. In such cases judgment should be delivered, not according to the letter of the law, but by recourse to equity, this being the intention of the lawgiver' (Q.60, art.5, ad.2). Therefore, St Thomas calls equity 'the principal form' of general justice, 'a kind of higher rule for human actions' (Q.120, art.2). It might well be called 'justice at full stretch'.

We shall see, when we consider the question of the just wage, how general (social) justice, commutative (exchange) justice and distributive justice come into play. It must be borne in mind that the categorization of kinds of justice is of no importance in itself. It is of use only to the extent that it helps us to see our duty more clearly and perform it more perfectly.

The just wage (paragraph 34)

Poverty is not a new problem. As Leo XIII pointed out, the Church has always met it with works of charity organized on the scale required to meet the needs. What he observed as new was the appearance of a great multitude of men who were miserably poor, not because they were unable to work, but because, work though they did and indeed excessively, they were not paid enough for their labour to enable them to live becomingly. Leo argued that this situation could be put right only by acts of justice.

The immediate questions that arise are: Why did Leo think that more income was due to the working labourer in justice rather than in charity? And, if there was a claim in justice, under what category of justice did the claim arise? Or, putting it another way, given that a debt existed, who owed it, how much was owed and why was it owed?

The teaching of the Church is that God gives the earth for the use of all mankind. This means that ordinarily all men shall have an opportunity to gain what they need either from their own property or by working on the property of others. When, as was the case in the industrialized and industrializing Europe of Leo's day, society is divided between a small minority of rich employers who own the capital and a large majority of poor employees who have only their labour whereby they can live, God's purpose can be served only if the employers provide work enough at wages high enough to enable the people, *proletarii*, to provide for their needs. When there is widespread failure to do this there is failure to secure the common good; and where there is such a failure there is a failure of *general (social) justice*, which directs men to the common good.

It is plain why Leo speaks of *natural justice* in para. 34. Its requirements arise out of the nature of things. God's providence requires from men arrangements which men have failed to make; and men may not defend themselves against the charge of injustice by blaming laws and institutions which they themselves have made. Those responsible had left the settlement of wage levels to the play of free competition in conditions where that did not exist and employers did not in fact compete with one another for the services of workers. Thus the employers could and did impose upon the workers a yoke little better than slavery. In acting thus they had set themselves against the providence of God. Speaking of the same matter in *Mater et magistra* (71) Pope John XXIII said that wages 'may not be settled arbitrarily by those who wield power'; and he used the word *fas*, divine law, to denote the source of the prohibition. By using their superior power to impose terms which the workers would not willingly have accepted the employers were guilty of offences against *exchange justice*. They were paying for the labour services less than the labour services were worth.

There was a failure also of *distributive justice*. Within its duty to provide for the common good by protecting conditions conducive to the life and happiness of every individual within its boundaries, the state ought to give particular attention to the needs of the weak. Pope Leo gives a long list of the measures which the state ought to take (27–28). It is to be noted particularly that the section which deals with wages falls within that part of the encyclical which is headed: 'The action of the state.'

As for the unpropertied workers, it is with their employers and not with the state that they make their contracts. It is for the good of the employers that they are engaged and it is out of the product of the businesses of their employers that they are paid. In the first instance, therefore, it is *exchange justice* and the duties of the employers in that virtue which is in question. Hence, the answer from Rome to the first question put by the Archbishop of Malines.

Pope Leo leaves us in no doubt of his judgment. He has been widely condemned (utterly unjustly) for putting defence of private property first in his analysis of what the needs of the time required; and yet he says bluntly (33) 'as regards protection of this world's goods, the first task is to save the wretched workers from the brutality of those who make use of human beings as mere instruments for the unrestrained acquisition of wealth.' He was convinced that the product of labour was enough to provide for wages substantially higher than were being paid; and that the employers, in their avariciousness, were using their superior strength to keep back from the workers what was not theirs to retain.

So we come to the question: How much was owed?

It appears to be generally agreed today that Leo's teaching was that the employer owed a 'family' wage, and this was the view of Pius XI. But it was by no means the general belief in 1891; and, as the Appendix shows, it was a view not held by men whom Rome thought well qualified to judge.

The text of the encyclical seems to leave little room for doubt that Pope Leo's answer was that the minimum owed by employer to an adult male worker (the case of the female we shall look at later) was what would suffice for 'the bodily needs of a temperate and well-behaved' man. He did not consider that the product of an unskilled labourer's work was, or in the nature of things ought to be, more than enough for his individual needs–which, let it be noted, covered more than bare subsistence.

In para. 34 Leo speaks expressly of the individual and makes no mention at all of family needs; and in para. 33 he takes it for granted that women and children also will be working for wages. All that he has to say about them is that they should not be asked to perform tasks which are beyond their physical capacity; that no child should be allowed into a factory who is not sufficiently mature for conditions there; and that women should be employed rather on tasks of a domestic type, which are more suited to their physical and emotional make-up and correspond with the tasks which most of them will anyway be performing for their families.

Against this, attention is drawn to Leo's remark in para. 35 that a man whose wage enables him 'to make ample provision for the needs of himself, his wife and his children' will find it easy to save; and it is argued from this that the Pope is satisfied that the minimum wage due in justice from the employer is such an 'ample' wage. The late Fr Lewis Watt S.J., an authority in his day, seems to have made this view his own in his *Catholic Social Principles* (p.44). Great as is the respect I have for the opinion of my old teacher and friend, it does seem to me that para. 35 will not bear this interpretation. In the context it seems to me to be clear that the Pope is simply continuing his argument for widespread property ownership. Having argued that this is essential, he now remarks that those workers who can do so should be encouraged to aspire to ownership. Great is the pity that the advice he gave that 'as many as possible of the people', 'the multitude', should be enabled to exercise ownership of means of production was ignored.

Further support of the view that Pope Leo argued for a family wage is sought in his remark (para. 10) that 'a most sacred law of nature ordains that the head of a family should provide for the necessities and comforts' of his children. This claim drags Leo's remark out of context. In para. 10 he is arguing that the right to private property is essential to the family, as true a society as the state and older than any state, if it is to fulfil its function, which is not the state's function but one which the state has a duty to protect.

A similar objection can be made to the argument that Pope Leo's remark in para. 33 that women 'are adapted rather to domestic tasks' indicated opposition on his part to women working for wages. It is surely obvious that in this context he is talking about women who are working for wages and about the tasks they are called upon to do in the course of their employment.

We must be careful to read *Rerum novarum* within the context of Leo's time and place. The whole of his life had been spent in a milieu where the wage-earning of the wives and children of the poor was taken for granted and always had been. He was obviously in touch with developments in northern Europe, but only through reports he received, not at all from personal experience; and although he was more discerning than the great majority of his contemporaries, many of them better placed than he was to appreciate what was going on, it would be surprising if he was aware of the full enormity of the state of affairs in the mill-towns and mining villages of Britain and Germany. His judgment of what action God's providence required of men owed more to what he personally knew of Italy than to what other men reported from elsewhere. We ought perhaps to remind ourselves of how much Pope Leo XIII was the product of a very different world and to recall that he had been a governor and magistrate in the Papal States and in that capacity had condemned men to death for brigandage. (It should be added, perhaps, that it was the leaders, from the local nobility, whom he had hanged. Their followers got off much more lightly.) Such a man could have been mistaken in his judgment of the actual situation and of the claims in justice to which it gave rise.

It seems to me that it is only by taking statements out of context that we can deny that Leo XIII believed that an individual wage was the unskilled working-man's due in exchange justice. If we believe that in his day a family wage was due it is better to say that Leo was mistaken in his opinion than to do violence to his text.

It could be that after Leo had published his encyclical and dispute arose he became uncertain himself. Otherwise, it might be argued, he would have taken the opportunity offered by his letter to Cardinal Goossens and the Belgian bishops in 1895 to clear up the point, instead of forbidding dissension about it.

We are left with the question of *distributive justice*. Despite the injury that was being done to wage-earners Leo did not consider that wage-fixing was a task for the state. Wages were a matter to be settled between the parties concerned, like any other price, and he wanted to be sure that the wage-earners could effectively bargain to get the wages their services warranted. This is not surprising. Catholic social teaching has always been that the consensus of the people who are actively engaged in the market place is the best guide to what is just, provided always that the strong there are prevented from cheating the weak. He did not rule out action by the state. Paragraphs 28 to 33 contain a long list of duties which the state should undertake in defence of the human rights of wage-earners and their families. These concern common objective standards which could be fixed, unlike wages, which of their nature vary from employment to employment and from time to time. For strengthening workers in their wage negotiations Leo looked to strong trade unions and a wider spread of property ownership.

There is nothing more to be said about the treatment of wages in *Rerum novarum*, but much to be said about developments since his day.

It was not long before opinion swung strongly against the justice of the individual wage as a minimum and in favour of the family wage. The argument for the family wage begins where Leo's argument for the individual wage began: the obligation that men have to establish such laws and institutions as will enable everybody to have access to the resources of nature on terms which do not of themselves deny the very purpose of those resources. The new element in wages doctrine is the insistence that this moral requirement cannot now be met in industrialized societies unless a man can earn enough for a family. If Leo XIII had been of that opinion he would have reached the same conclusion.

We see this development in the next major statement on wages in Pius XI's encyclical on marriage, *Casti connubii* (CTS Do 113, paras 122–128, pp.60–2). He says that all too often families are in such straitened circumstances that they find it extremely difficult to do their duty. It becomes necessary, therefore, to come to their aid 'in the best way possible'.

This way is, in the first instance, the payment of a family wage. 'Everything possible is to be done to bring about what Leo XIII had demanded: that economic and social affairs be so arranged that every head of a family should be able to earn and to acquire enough to provide for the needs of himself, his wife and his children, according to his place in society and the locality where he lives. To deny this or to consider less to be right and fair is a grave injustice which Scripture ranks among the greatest of sins.

If offends against divine law *(fas)* to fix wages below what, in relation to all the circumstances, is sufficient to provide for family needs.'

However, Pius XI took a stern view of the responsibility of the couple. People ought to prepare for the financial burdens of marriage and be helped to do so; and if they find that they cannot provide for themselves they ought to combine with others of like kind to make provision for whatever is necessary through joint efforts in private and public associations.

It is only when these efforts fail, particularly with large families and with couples who are unable to manage their income, that outside help is to be looked for. In the first instance it is for Christian charity to make up to the poor what they lack. When even this is not enough it becomes the duty of the state to make up what is wanting. 'Those who have charge of the state and the common good cannot neglect the material wants of married couples and of families without doing grave damage to the commonwealth and the common good. They have a major duty to make laws and arrange public spending so as to put the care of poor families in the forefront of policy.'

The view taken of the family wage is a modest one. It appears to be not related to the needs of large families; and even those of smaller size are supposed to provide out of savings for part of the burden of a family at its peak or, should savings fail, make provision through some sort of friendly society. Help from outside, whether it be by charity or by state provision, is to be looked for only when properly organized self-help fails. State provision has to be generous, but it is a last resort.

By the time Pius XI came to write *Quadragesimo anno* a year later the emphasis of his thinking had shifted somewhat (paras 65–76). He is even more insistent upon the priority to be given to the upbringing of children. 'Intolerable and at all costs to be abolished is the abuse whereby mothers of families, because of the insufficiency of the father's salary, are forced to engage in gainful occupations outside the domestic walls, to the neglect of their own proper cares and duties, particularly the upbringing of their children.' It is not that he objected to mothers working for wages. He says expressly that it is right for wives and children to contribute to the family income 'according to their power'. His objection was to their having to go out to work under conditions which forced them to neglect a major obligation with a consequent failure of the family to perform its social function. Industrialization which makes it impossible for wives and mothers to work for wages without this effect ought not to be undertaken unless by its means a man's productivity can be raised high enough to enable him to earn at least as much as his family earned before industrialization. An increase in national product –in itself a desirable good (*Rerum novarum*, 26)–can be bought at too high a cost.

Industrialization has taken place and is still taking place under conditions which fail to satisfy this test. Whereas Leo XIII was confident that the social economy of his day was productive enough to make an individual living wage a requirement of commutative (exchange) justice, Pius XI and his successors have not been at all certain that the social economies of their day could do the same for a family living wage. Hence they put emphasis upon a requirement of social (general) justice. As Pius XI puts it in *Quadragesimo anno* (72): 'Every effort must therefore be made that fathers of families receive a wage sufficient to meet adequately normal *(communis)* domestic needs. If under present circumstances this is not always feasible, social justice demands that reforms be introduced without delay which will guarantee such a wage to every adult working man.'

That every adult working man is to have a family wage indicates that the reforms called for cannot consist in the introduction of family allowances. The Pope is speaking of the value of a worker's service, not of the extent of his need.

Pius XI draws attention to three fields in which reforms can be undertaken.

Firstly, there is a possibility that managements are inefficient or idle or insufficiently innovative. Such managements must not be allowed to pay low wages. Every employer owes to a worker what that worker's service would be worth in the hands of a competent manager. John XXIII enlarges on this in a letter which Cardinal Cicognani sent on his behalf to the Spanish social study week of 1962: 'A Christian employer ought to think himself gravely obliged to use every available means–as by changing his methods of production or completely re-equipping his enterprise –to make it possible for him to pay what is due in justice to his workers for their work' (Utz, *Doctrine*, XX, 104).

Secondly, governments or other agencies which impose unjust burdens on a business or compel it to sell at prices which do not cover costs are guilty of grievous wrong, for it is they who deprive the workers of a just wage. This remark about a single business reinforces what the Pope has already said in para. 70 about the duties of governments in support of a prosperous economy, duties of which Leo XIII speaks in *Rerum novarum* (26).

Pius XI draws attention also to the danger of having a general level of wages which is either too low or too high in relation to productivity, since either can cause otherwise avoidable unemployment, and to the need to ensure that wages in different parts of the economy are kept in balance. 'To raise or lower wages unduly, with a view to private advantage and with no consideration for the common good, is contrary to social justice.' Later Pius XII was to condemn employers who profited from unemployment by 'cutting wages to an intolerably low level' (Utz, *Relations*, no.1914).

Given his strong insistence on the subsidiary function of the state, we can be sure that Pius XI is not proposing a wide extension of government intervention in industry and trade. We have no reason to suppose that he disagrees with Pope Leo's view that these matters lie primarily within the domain of associations of employers and of workers (*Rerum novarum*, 34). The state has a duty to intervene only when other social agencies fail and the common good is endangered.

Thirdly, in the last resort when a business cannot pay a just wage thought should be given to its closure and the making of other provision for its employees. It is of interest to note that Pius XI does not suggest that such a business be kept going by means of subsidies. His interest is in getting the value of labour services – i.e. their productivity – up; and continued employment in unprofitable undertakings is not the way to do that.

So far the teaching of Pius XI on wages is clear. However, in the course of his argument he appears to introduce a note of confusion.

In *Casti connubii* he uses the word 'wage' in relation only to what the worker earns or, more accurately, ought to be able to earn. It is not used of the help from whatever source which must be given to families in distress. In *Quadragesimo anno* the distinction between earnings and aid is dropped. It can be argued that this use of language conforms to that of the worker who regards whatever is in his pay-packet as his wage and does not much bother to distinguish between its component parts, except on what touches bonus or overtime. Nevertheless, discussion does tend to become confused when the same word is used to signify both what is due in commutative justice and what is due in distributive justice. Since the publication of *Quadragesimo anno*, 'wage' can mean either that which will suffice for 'normal' family needs and which every adult man ought to be able to earn, or a payment which increases as family burdens increase above the 'normal'.

Thus, we find Pius XII saying to representatives of family organizations: 'In their social messages the popes have always spoken firmly of the family or social wage *(salaire familial ou social)* which permits the family to provide for the increasing needs of their children as they grow up' (20 September 1949: *AAS 1949*, p.553; Utz, *Relations*, no.2816). John XXIII uses *merces* in the same way in *Mater et magistra* (71) and in *Pacem in terris* (20), although in the latter case with a cautionary 'having regard to the resources available'. Writing to the Spaniards via Cardinal Cicognani, he spoke of *la justa retribución del trabajo* which would provide for a seemly life for a family (Utz, *Doctrine*, XX, 102).

If we look only at these and similar statements we get the impression that papal teaching has abandoned the proposition that the employment relationship arises out of a contract which is governed by commutative justice; i.e. that the wage owed by an employer to an employee for a service rendered is the exchange value of that service, its price. That there has been no such abandonment is shown by the way in which Pius XII deals with the relationship which ought to obtain between the wages of men and of women; and with the argument that a business is a society of which the wage-earners are members in such a way as gives them entitlement to a share in the profits.

Speaking to Italian working-women Pius XII was forthright on the first issue. 'We have no need to remind you, who have much experience in social affairs, how the Church has always upheld the principle that to the working-woman who gives the same service with the same productivity as that given by a man is due the same wage *(la stessa mercede)* as is given to a man; and how unjust and contrary to the common good it would be to exploit the labour of women simply because it can be had at a lower price' (*AAS 1945*, p.214; a French version is in Utz, *Relations*, no. 3271).

Pius XII dealt with the second issue in a speech to members of UNIAPAC, 'It would be a mistake to affirm that every particular enterprise is by its nature a society in such sort that the relationships between those who participate in it are governed by the rules of distributive justice, so that all without distinction—whether or not they own the means of production—should have a right to their share of the property or at least of the profits of the enterprise' (*AAS 1949*, p.285).

The meaning is clear: at the level of the enterprise it is commutative justice which governs the exchange between employer and employed.

We appear to be faced with contradictory statements. However, regrettable though the ambiguous use of language is, the contradiction is only apparent. It is cleared up if we go back to first principles.

All men have a right of access to the use of the goods of the earth on terms which fully respect their human dignity. In a social economy where large numbers of people have no means other than the sale of their labour whereby they can live, it must be made possible for them to live by that means becomingly. If the techniques of production are such that wives and mothers cannot contribute to the family income by working for wages without neglecting their domestic duties, it must be made possible for heads of families to earn enough to provide for the family needs. When a man gives to the economy, via an employer, the full use of the only asset he possesses, his labour, it is right so to arrange affairs that he receives in return sufficient for his needs. There is a link between the labour of the working-man and the obligations of a society larger than that of the business which employs him.

Thus, speaking to Italian Catholic trade unionists, Pius XII urged them to stop using 'empty phrases' and to make the thinking of *Quadragesimo anno* their own. 'Beyond the distinction between employers and employed, men ought to be able to discern that higher unity which binds together all those who collaborate in production; that is to say, their fellowship and solidarity in their joint task of making regular provision for the common good and the needs of all in the community.' Thanks to this harmonious co-operation 'the worker will come to obtain stable earnings *(un guadagno tranquillo)* sufficient for the upkeep of his family' (*AAS 1945*, pp.71–72; a French version is in Utz, *Relations*, no.3056).

Employers and workers are united not only in contributing to the output of the economy but also in sharing in its fruits. 'They eat at the same table, since in the final analysis it is from the net national income that they get their living. Each one draws his income and when we consider their relations in this way we see that neither party is at the service of the other. Receipt of income is an entitlement *(Toucher son revenu est un apanage)* which belongs to the personal dignity of whomever, in one way or another, whether as employer or as worker, makes his contribution to the product of the national economy. In the balance sheet of the undertaking wages appear as a cost to the employer. But in the national economy there is only one kind of cost, the material goods which are used up in the course of production and which have to be continually replaced' (Pius XII to UNIAPAC: *AAS 1949*, p.283; Utz, *Relations*, nos.3487–3489).

In these two passages Pius XII provides us with the solution to the apparent confusion created by the use the popes have made of the one word 'wage' to signify both the worker's cost to the employer and the worker's share in the joint national product. When he engages the services of workers an employer will be led to making a truly economical use of scarce human resources if he pays for each service a price which answers to the contribution that service makes to the output of his business; that is to say, when he pays to workers what is due to them in commutative justice. In this way he serves the common good. But when we look at wages through the other end of the telescope, so to speak, we perceive that they constitute the principal, if not the only, means by which workers can receive the income which is their due. Hence Pius XI's remark in *Divini redemptoris* (51): 'It is not right that the worker should receive as alms what is due to him in justice.'

This argument is more fully developed in the encyclical *Laborem exercens* which was published by Pope John Paul II to celebrate the ninetieth anniversary of *Rerum novarum* (paras 72–81, 88–90). The Pope begins by pointing out that a man has a duty to work for his own family, but also for the nation 'which is his mother' and for the 'whole human family of which he is a member'. He benefits from the work of past generations and in turn bequeaths a legacy to people yet to be born. 'All this constitutes the moral obligation to work . . . consequently, when we consider the moral rights of every man with regard to work . . . we must always keep before our eyes the vast range of conditions and circumstances which provides the context of the labour of every working-man.'

This consideration leads the Pope to make a distinction between the *direct* and the *indirect employer*. The direct employer is 'the person or institution with whom the worker enters directly into a contract of employment'. The indirect employer is constituted by the 'many other distinct elements which exercise a definite influence upon the way in which the contract of employment is agreed upon or the more or less just working relationships are established'.

He then proceeds to point out that a 'key problem of social ethics is equitable remuneration for work done' and that 'in today's conditions payment for work *(remuneratio operis)* has more importance than anything else for establishing a just relationship between employer and employed'. The indirect employer has an important part to play, but the wage relationship is 'first and foremost' the concern of the direct employer.

Having said this, the Pope proceeds at once to point out that the justice of a social economy has to be judged 'by the way in which provision is made for fair payment for a man's work' in obedience to 'the first principle of the entire ethico-social order, the universal use of goods'. However capital and labour are related, 'the payment made for work, the wage *(merces)*, remains the practical means by which the vast majority of people can have access to the goods intended for everybody's use'. Hence, 'a just wage is always the concrete verification of a whole social economy and of its proper functioning'.

'This test of justice especially concerns the family. Just payment for the work of an adult, on whom falls responsibility for a family, will be expressly that which suffices for founding and properly maintaining a family and providing securely for its future.' That sort of payment can be made either by 'one single wage, paid to the head of the family, which is sufficient to provide for the needs of the family and so leaves his wife under no necessity to take a job outside the home; or by means of other social measures, such as family allowances or grants to mothers who devote themselves exclusively to their families'.

The popes see a man's work and therefore his claim to remuneration in relation to a whole social economy as well as to the business in which it is located. It is through this work that the worker ought to expect to receive access to the goods which are meant for the use of everybody and which have been produced by joint efforts, because he has played his part in those efforts. It is true that at the level of the business and bearing its social purpose in mind the paramount concern of the direct employer has to be the value of the labour service to the business; but at the level of the economy and bearing its purpose in mind the paramount concern to the indirect employer must be the satisfaction of the needs of the workers and their families.

The popes are anxious to see maintained the link between the rendering of labour service and the receipt by the labourer of income sufficient for family needs. Reallocation of income from those with more than they need to those with less is best done in a way which recognizes the co-operative character of production and allows the worker to perceive the connection between his family's living standard and the contribution he makes by his labour. This is best done when the family income appears in the worker's pay-packet. It is probably for this reason that the popes show a strong preference for the 'family wage' even though they do not condemn payments made to the mother of a family. In terms of this argument 'wage' can be used legitimately in the two senses: the payment which is due in commutative justice from the direct employer and that which is due in distributive justice from the indirect employer.

As with Leo XIII so also with Pius XII there is a deep distrust of actual governments. The popes are ever aware that although political authority comes from God it is wielded by men who often mistake its purpose. Whenever they discuss economic matters, therefore, they are careful to exclude the state from any activity which can be carried on by some lesser body.

Thus, we have Pius XII, speaking to members of UNIAPAC, reminding them that 'it is the task of public right to serve private right and not to absorb it. No more than any other branch of human activity is the economy of its nature an institution of the state. On the contrary, it is the living product of the free initiative of individuals and of the groups which they freely form' (*AAS 1949*, p.285; Utz, *Relations*, no.3491).

It is no cause for surprise, therefore, to find the same Pope, writing to the 1952 French social study week on the theme

'Riches and Poverty', pointing to the proper sphere of the state in economic matters and expressing his fear lest 'abuses of collective security should infringe the rights of the person and the family' (Utz, *Relations*, no.3542). It is for this reason that in his speech to UNIAPAC the Pope emphasized the need for institutions publicly recognized but privately instituted, which would be 'founded precisely on the community of responsibility between all those who are engaged in production' *(loc. cit.)*. The lesson is plain: men who are engaged in industry and trade ought to be able to look to the economy and not to the state for their income. That is their *apanage*, their entitlement.

The popes fear lest the state be permitted to take upon itself duties which families and lesser groups can undertake for themselves if only their incomes be sufficient *(Rerum novarum*, 29; *Quadragesimo anno*, 79). It is wrong to make lack of income an excuse for taking away from families functions which are properly theirs. Thus we have Pius XII speaking to members of the International Union of Family Organizations: 'It is unfortunately only too true that in today's economic and social conditions the family which is reduced to dependence upon its own resources, which has no other help and no other support, which is isolated and simply one among many others, may be in no position to look after itself and still less to play its part as an organic and living cell. But that is not reason for bringing to it a remedy which is worse than the disease . . . material or moral subjection which, as regards the education of their children, reduces parents almost to the condition of convicted criminals who have forfeited their parental authority. The idea of the family as it exists in the sight of God makes necessary a return to the one principle on which a good answer can be based: to make use of every means to put the family into a position where it can both attend to its own needs and make its contribution to the common good' (*AAS 1949*, pp.552–553; Utz, *Relations*, nos. 2812, 2815).

It must be emphasized that when the popes are speaking of provision for family needs it is the families of poor labouring men that they have in mind. All agree with Leo XIII: the well-to-do can be left to look after themselves (*Rerum novarum*, 29). It is particularly with the wives of poor working-men who themselves have to work for wages that the popes are concerned. Thus we have Pius XII speaking to a group of Italian working-women: 'All that the Church does in favour of a wage which will provide for the maintenance of the worker and his family has had and continues to have precisely this aim (very often difficult to attain) of bringing back the wife and mother to her proper vocation in the home.' It is to enable 'you to make your home, in the words of St Paul (1 Tim. 2:2), a place where people "May be able to live religious and reverent lives in peace and quiet"' (*AAS 1945*, pp.213–214: a French version is in Utz, *Relations*, nos. 3269–3270).

In the minds of the popes, then, there is no question of provision for men whose earnings in commutative justice are sufficient for the maintenance of their families. Need is the paramount consideration as regards the part to be played in wages payments by the indirect employer. Family allowances available to everybody are not what the popes are speaking and writing about.

There remains one last point. The existence of a substantial number of low wage earners (direct employer) is not in itself proof of a major defect in a social economy. Such may be the case. For example, there may be a shortage of skilled workers which keeps down the employment and the output and pay of unskilled workers. But however well an economy be organized there will always be some men who for one reason or another are incapable of a work performance which will earn them from their direct employers a wage at the going rate—as Luis de Molina and John de Lugo recognized (cf. above, pp.38–9). Their incomes have to be supplemented. General wage increases from their direct employers are not an appropriate remedy for their plight.